Beatles In Their Own Words.

Compiled by Miles.
Edited by Pearce Marchbank.
Designed by Perry Neville.

Omnibus Press
London/New York/Sydney

Introduction.
Page 6.

Beatles: The Story.
Page 9.

Press Conferences.
Page 47.

Songwriting.
Page 71.

The Songs.
Page 79.

The Films.
Page 107.

Drugs.
Page 115.

Politics.
Page 123.

Exclusive distributors:
Book Sales Limited, 8/9 Frith Street, London,
W1V 5TZ, England.
Music Sales Pty. Limited, 120 Rothschild
Avenue, Rosebery, NSW2018, Australia.
To the Music Trade:
Music Sales Corporation,
257 Park Avenue South, New York,
NY 10010, USA

Art director: Pearce Marchbank
Cover photograph: L.F.I.

Photo credits: pages 2, 16, 18, 19, 56, 100
& 128 courtesy Beat Publications Limited;
pages 5, 6, 12, 21, 23, 26, 30, 37, 38, 48,
50, 55, 60, 63, 65, 83, 85, 90, 94, 106, 108,
126 courtesy Rex Features; pages 34, 40,
42, 46, 68, 72, 104, 111 courtesy
Camera Press.

This book © copyright 1978 Omnibus Press
(A division of Book Sales Limited)

Introduction © copyright 1978 Barry Miles

Library of Congress Catalogue No. 78-56240
ISBN 0.86001.540.8
UK Order No. OP 40419
US Order No. 030925

Printed and bound in Great Britain
by Page Bros, Norwich

A catalogue record for this title is available from
the British Library.

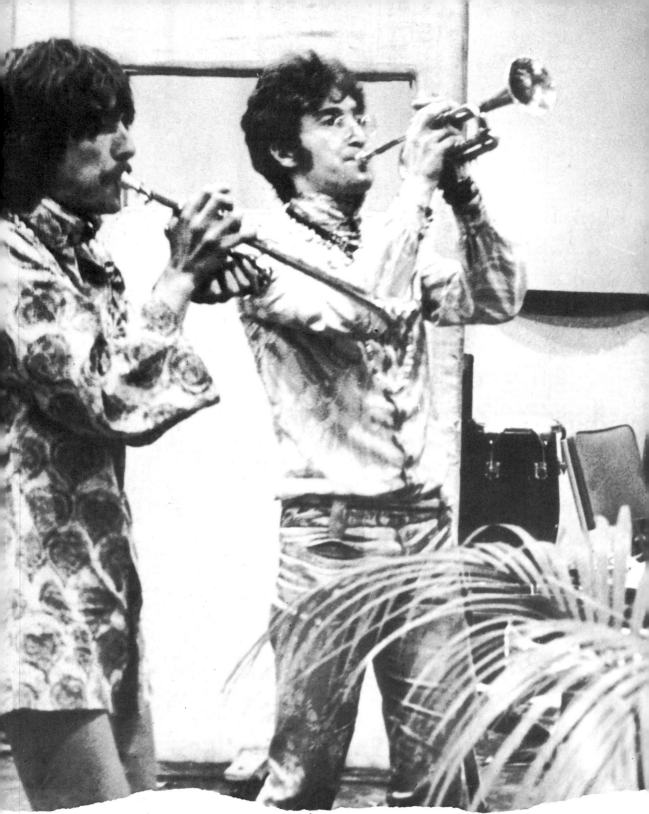

The material in this book is taken from an extensive file of
interviews and clippings assembled by the compiler over the years.
The sources are too diverse to list separately, even if all of them
were known. Most of the short quotes and one-liners are taken

from press conferences in New York City and London from
the very early days. Many of the longer quotes from McCartney,
Lennon and Harrison come from interviews done in 1966 and
1968 by the compiler. *Miles*.

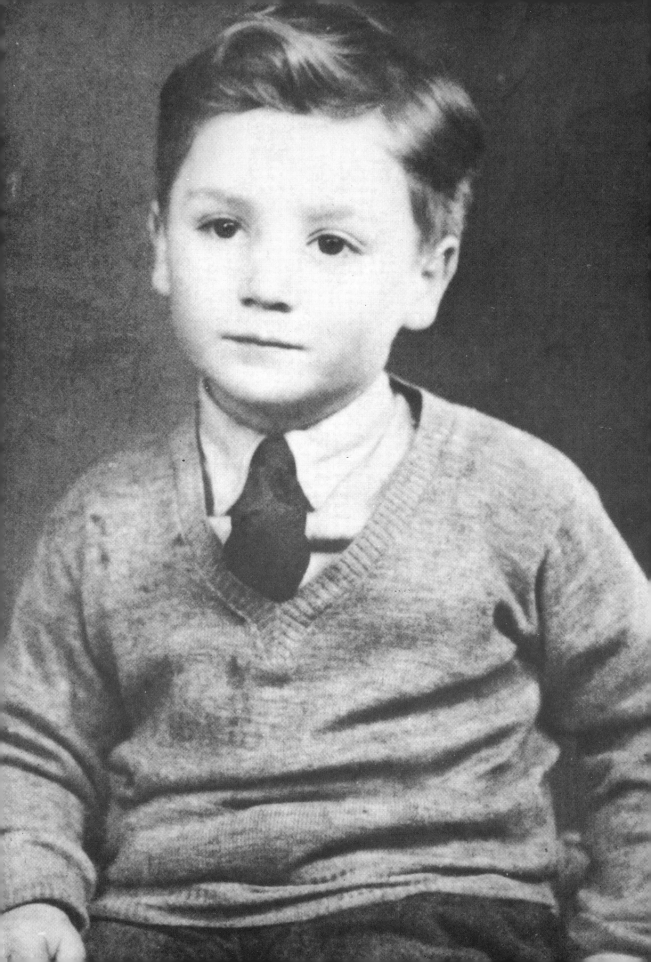

Beatles: The Story.

John Lennon: I remember the first guitar I ever saw. It belonged to a guy in a cowboy suit in a province of Liverpool, with stars, and a cowboy hat and a big dobro. They were real cowboys, and they took it seriously. There had been cowboys long before there was rock and roll.

John Lennon: People like me are aware of their so-called genius at ten, eight, nine . . . I always wondered, why has nobody discovered me? In school, didn't they see that I'm cleverer than anybody in this school? That the teachers are stupid, too? That all they had was information that I didn't need.

I got fuckin' lost in being at high school. I used to say to me auntie, "You throw my fuckin' poetry out, and you'll regret it when I'm famous," and she threw the bastard stuff out.

I never forgave her for not treating me like a fuckin' genius or whatever I was, when I was a child.

It was obvious to me. Why didn't they put me in art school? Why didn't they train me? Why would they keep forcing me to be a fuckin' cowboy like the rest of them? I was different, I was always different. Why didn't anybody notice me?

A couple of teachers would notice me, encourage me to be something or other, to draw or to paint — express myself. But most of the time they were trying to beat me into being a fuckin' dentist or a teacher. And then the fuckin' fans tried to beat me into being a fuckin' Beatle or an Engelbert Humperdinck, and the critics tried to beat me into being Paul McCartney.

John Lennon: I went to see *Rock Around The Clock* and I was most surprised. Nobody was screaming and nobody was dancing. I mean, I had read that everybody danced in the aisles. It must have all been done before I went. I was all set to tear up the seats too, but nobody joined in.

Paul McCartney: I wanted to do something in music and my dad gave me a trumpet, for my birthday. I went through trying to learn that. But my mouth used to get too sore. You know, you have to go through a period of gettin' your lip hard. I suddenly realized I wouldn't be able to sing if I played trumpet. So I figured guitar would be better. It was about the time that guitar was beginning to be *the* instrument. So I went and swapped my trumpet for a guitar and I got that home and couldn't figure out what was wrong and I suddenly decided to turn the strings around and that made a difference and I realized I was left-handed. I started from there, really; that was my first kind of thing, and then once you had a guitar you were then kind of eligible for bands and stuff. But I never thought of myself being in a band.

One day I went with this friend of mine. His name was Ivan [Vaughn]. And I went up to Woolton, in Liverpool, and there was a village fete on, and John and his friends were playing for the thing. My friend Ivan knew John, who was a neighbour of his. And we met there and John was onstage singing "Come little darlin', come and go with me . . ."

But he never knew the words because he didn't know the record, so he made up his own words, like "Down, down, down, down, to the penitentiary." I remember I was impressed. I thought, wow, he's good. That's a good band there. So backstage, back in the church hall later, I was singing a couple of songs I'd known.

I used to know all the words to 'Twenty Flight Rock' and a few others and it was pretty much in those days to know the words to that. John didn't know the words to many songs. So I was valuable. I wrote up a few words and showed him how to play 'Twenty Flight Rock' and another one, I think. He played all this stuff and I remember thinking he smelled a bit drunk. Quite a nice chap, but he was still a bit drunk. Anyway, that was my first introduction, and I sang a couple of old things.

I liked their band, and then one of their friends who was in the band, a guy called Pete Shotton who was a friend of John's, saw me cycling up in Woolton one day and said, "Hey, they said they'd quite like to have you in the band, if you'd like to join". I said, "Oh, yeah, it'd be great". We then met up somewhere and I was in the band.

I was originally on guitar. The first thing we had was at a Conservative Club somewhere in Broadway, which is an area of Liverpool, as well as New York. There was a Conservative Club there and I had a big solo, a guitar boogie. I had this big solo and it came to my bit and I blew it. I blew it. Sticky fingers, you know. I couldn't play at all and I got terribly embarrassed. So I goofed that one terribly, so from then on I was on rhythm guitar. Blown out on lead!

We went to Hamburg, and I had a real cheap guitar, an electric guitar. It finally blew up on me, it finally fell apart in Hamburg. It just wasn't used to being used like that. Then I was on piano for a little while. So I went from bass to lead guitar to rhythm guitar to piano. I used to do a few numbers like Ray Charles' 'Don't Let the Sun Catch You Crying' and a couple of Jerry Lee Lewis' like 'High School Confidential'.

Then Stuart [Sutcliffe] left the group. He was the bass player. He lent me his bass, and I

PAUL McCARTNEY

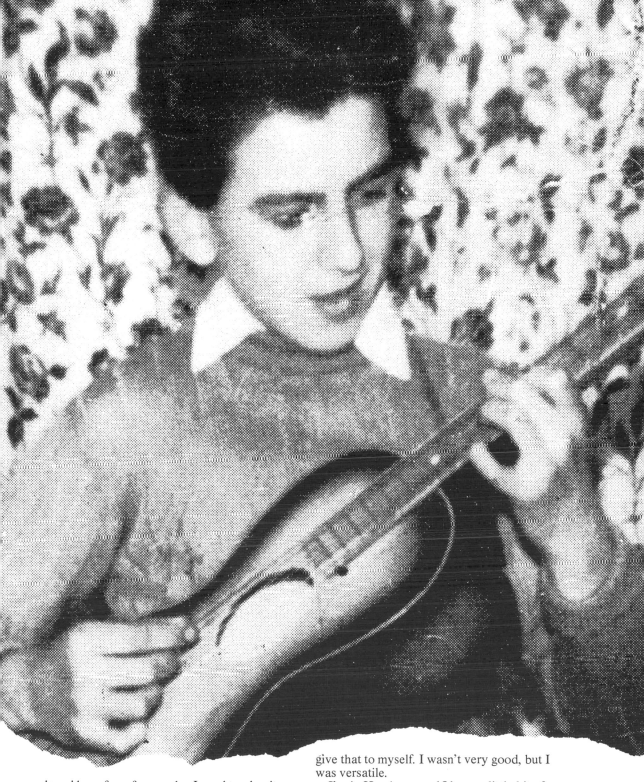

played bass for a few weeks. I used to play it upside down. And he used to have piano strings on it, because you couldn't get bass strings. They were a bit rare, you know, and they cost a lot, too, about £2 for one string. So he would cut these big lengths of piano strings from the piano and wind them on this guitar. So I played that upside down for a while. I'm pretty versatile, I'll give that to myself. I wasn't very good, but I was versatile.

I'm in Hamburg, and I have a little bit of money together, and finally saved enough money to buy myself a Hoffman violin bass. It was my bass, then, that was the one. And I became known for that bass, a lot of kids got them. That was my big pride and joy, because it sounded great.

And that was it, basically.

STU SUTCLIFFE & ASTRID

RINGC STARR

John Lennon: I had a group, I was the singer and the leader; I met Paul and I made a decision whether to — and he made a decision too — have him in the group: was it better to have a guy who was better than the people I had in, obviously, or not? To make the group stronger or to let me be stronger? That decision was to let Paul in and make the group stronger.

Well, from that, Paul introduced me to George, and Paul and I had to make the decision, or I had to make the decision, whether to let George in. I listened to George play, and I said 'Play Raunchy' or whatever the old story is, and I let him in. I said 'OK, you come in'. That was the three of us then. Then the rest of the group was thrown out gradually. It just happened like that, instead of going for the individual thing, we went for the strongest format, and for equals.

George is ten years younger than me, or some shit like that. I couldn't be bothered with him when he first came around. He used to follow me around like a bloody kid, hanging around all the time, I couldn't be bothered. He was a kid who played guitar, and he was a friend of Paul's which made it all easier. It took me years to come around to him, to start considering him as an equal or anything.

We had all sorts of different drummers all the time, because people who owned drum kits were few and far between: it was an expensive item. They were usually idiots. Then we got Pete Best, because we needed a drummer to go to Hamburg the next day. We passed the audition on our own with a stray drummer. There are other myths about Pete Best was the Beatles and Stuart Sutcliffe's mother is writing in England that *he* was the Beatles.

John Lennon: In the beginning it was a constant fight between Brian [Epstein] and Paul on one side, and me and George on the other.

Brian put us in neat suits and shirts, and Paul was right behind him.

I didn't dig that, and I used to try and get George to rebel with me. I'd say to him: "Look, we don't need these fucking suits. Let's chuck them out of the window."

My little rebellion was to have my tie loose, with the top button of my shirt undone, but Paul'd always come up to me and put it straight.

I saw a film the other night, the first television film we ever did. The Granada people came down to film us, and there we were in suits and everything — it just wasn't us, and watching that film I knew that that was where we started to sell out.

John Lennon: We were performers — in spite of what Mick says about us — in Liverpool, Hamburg and other dance halls. What we generated was fantastic, when we played straight rock, and there was nobody to touch us in Britain. As soon as we made it, we made it, but the edges were knocked off.

You know Brian put us in suits and all that, and we made it very, very big. But we sold out, you know. The music was dead before we even went on the theatre tour of Britain. We were feeling shit already, because we had to reduce an hour or two hours' playing, which we were glad about in one way, to 20 minutes, and we would go on and repeat the same 20 minutes every night.

The Beatles music died then, as musicians. That's why we never improved as musicians; we killed ourselves then to make it. And that was the end of it. George and I are more inclined to say that; we always missed the club dates because that's when we were playing music, and then

PETE BEST

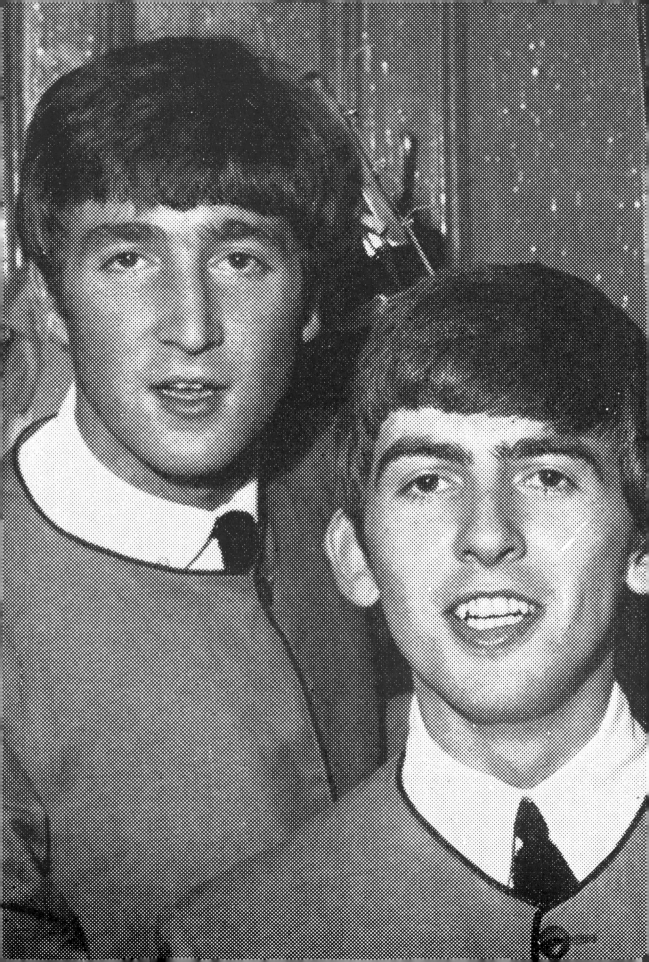

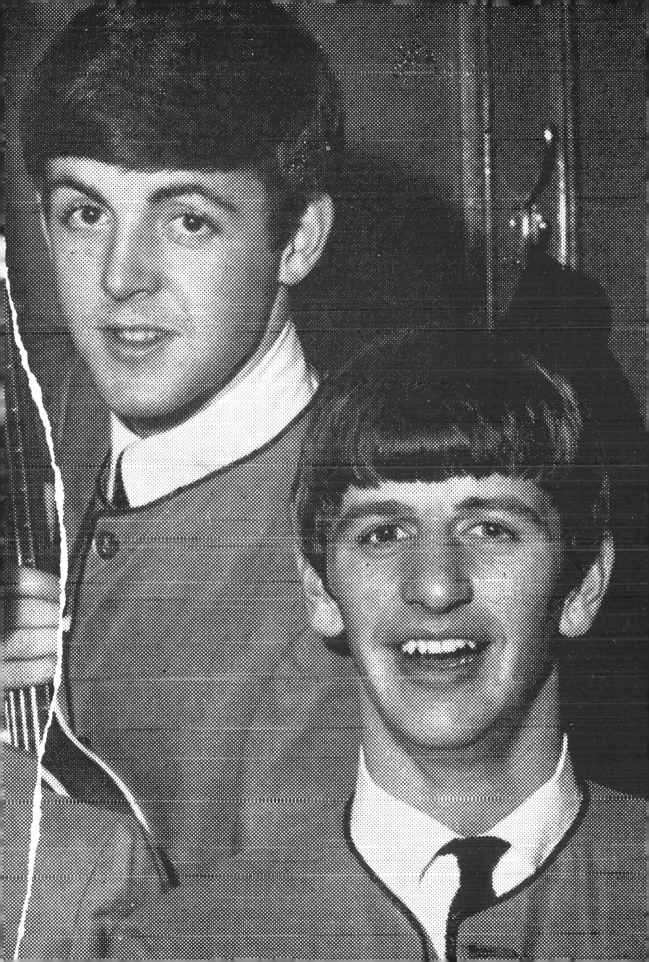

later on we became technically, efficient recording artists — which was another thing — because we were competent people and whatever media you put us in we can produce something worthwhile.

Ringo Starr: I started to be an engineer but I banged me thumb the first day. I became a drummer because it was the only thing I could do. But whenever I hear another drummer I know I'm no good. John learned me the song I sing. I can only play on the off beat because John can't keep up on the rhythm guitar. I'm no good on the technical things but I'm good with all the motions, swinging my head, like. That's because I love to dance but you can't do that on drums.

I remember when I first met the boys in Hamburg. Everybody used to talk about them because they did things like John going on stage with a toilet seat around his neck. They were living in an empty cinema called the Bambi which they called "The Pit". I was living at a hotel, because I was with a group called the Raving Texans.

Back in Liverpool, whenever Pete Best would get sick I would take over. Sometimes it was at lunch time. I remember once Neil got me out of bed and I had no kit. I got up on stage with only cymbals and gradually Pete's kit started arriving piece by piece.

I figure we're good for another four years. I don't want to invest me money in stocks or anything. I just want to have it and draw twenty or thirty quid a week. The main thing is, I don't ever want to go back to work.

I don't want to boast but when we were playing in Liverpool I was one of the two best drummers in town. We used to play for ten bob a night. I don't think I could ever do that again.

John Lennon and Paul McCartney on Dick Rowe, the A&R man for Decca Records who turned down the Beatles...
Paul: He must be kicking himself now.
John: I hope he kicks himself to death.
Paul: I don't blame him for turning us down.

George Martin: Listen to this tape playback and tell me if there's anything you don't like.
George: Well, I don't like your tie for a start.

John Lennon: That was a great period. We were like kings of the jungle then, and we were very close to the Stones. I don't know how close the others were but I spent a lot of time with Brian and Mick. I admire them, you know. I dug them the first time I saw them in whatever that place is they came from, Richmond. I spent a lot of time with them, and it was great. We all used to just go around London in cars and meet each other and talk about music with the Animals and

THE BEATLES WITH GEORGE MARTIN

Eric and all that. It was really a good time, that was the best period, fame-wise. We didn't get mobbed so much. It was like a men's smoking club, just a very good scene. Brian Jones was different over the years as he disintegrated. He ended up the kind of guy that you dread when he would come on the phone, because you knew it was trouble. He was really in a lot of pain. In the early days, he was all right, because he was young and confident. He was one of them guys that disintegrated in front of you. He wasn't sort of brilliant or anything, he was just a nice guy.

The Beatles tours were like the Fellini film *Satyricon*. We had that image. Man, our tours were like something else, if you could get on our tours, you were in. They were Satyricon, all right.

Wherever we went, there was always a whole scene going, we had our four separate bedrooms. We tried to keep them out of our room. Derek's and Neil's rooms were always full of junk and whores and who-the-fuck-knows-what, and policemen with it. Satyricon! We had to do something. What do you do when the pill doesn't wear off and it's time to go? I used to be up all night with Derek, whether there was anybody there or not, I could never sleep, such a heavy scene it was. They didn't call them groupies then, they called it something else and if we couldn't get groupies, we would have whores and everything, whatever was going.

When we hit town, we hit it. There was no pissing about. There's photographs of me crawling about in Amsterdam on my knees coming out of whore houses and things like that. The police escorted me to the places, because they never wanted a big scandal, you see. I don't really want to talk about it, because it will hurt Yoko. And it's not fair. Suffice to say, that they were Satyricon on tour and that's it, because I don't want to hurt their feelings, or the other people's girls either. It's just not fair.

Paul McCartney on the plane to NYC, talking to Phil Spector...
Paul: Since America has always had everything why should we be over there making money? They've got their own groups. What are we going to give them that they don't already have?

To the wine waiter at the 21 in NYC...
Ringo: Do you have any vintage Coca Cola?

After a show in the Washington Coliseum...
Ringo: Some of them even threw jelly babies in bags and they hurt like hailstones but they could have ripped me apart and I couldn't have cared less. What an audience! I could have played for them all night!

John Lennon: Oh sure. I dug the fame, the power, the money, and playing to big crowds.

Conquering America was the best thing.

You see we wanted to be bigger than Elvis — that was the main thing. At first we wanted to be Goffin and King, then we wanted to be Eddie Cochran, then we wanted to be Buddy Holly, and finally we arrived at wanting to be bigger than the biggest — and that was Elvis.

We reckoned we could make it because there were four of us. None of us would've made it alone, because Paul wasn't quite strong enough, I didn't have enough girl-appeal, George was too quiet, and Ringo was the drummer. But we thought that everyone would be able to dig at least one of us, and that's how it turned out.

John Lennon: We were really professional by the time we got to the States; we had learned the whole game. When we arrived here we knew how to handle the press; the British press were the toughest in the world and we could handle anything. We were all right.

On the plane over, I was thinking "Oh, we won't make it", or I said it on a film or something, but that's that side of me. We knew we would wipe you out if we could just get a grip on you. We were new.

And when we got here, you were all walking around in fuckin' Bermuda shorts, with Boston crew cuts and stuff on your teeth. Now they're telling us, they're all saying, Beatles are *passé* and this is like that, man. The chicks looked like fuckin' 1940 horses. There was no conception of dress or any of that jazz. We just thought "What an ugly race", it looked just disgusting. We thought how hip we were, but, of course, we weren't. It was just the five of us, us and the Stones were really the hip ones; the rest of England were just the same as they ever were.

You tend to get nationalistic, and we would really laugh at America, except for its music. It was the black music we dug, and over here even the blacks were laughing at people like Chuck Berry and the blues singers; the blacks thought it wasn't sharp to dig the really funky music, and the whites only listened to Jan and Dean and all that. We felt that we had the message which was "Listen to this music". It was the same in Liverpool, we felt very exclusive and underground in Liverpool, listening to Richie Barret and Barrett Strong, and all those old-time records. Nobody was listening to any of them except Eric Burdon in Newcastle and Mick Jagger in London. It was that lonely, it was fantastic. When we came over here and it was the same — nobody was listening to rock and roll or to black music in America — we felt as though we were coming to the land of its origin but nobody wanted to know about it.

John Lennon: The bigger we got, the more unreality we had to face; the more we were expected to do until, when you didn't sort of

shake hands with a Mayor's wife, she would start abusing you and screaming and saying "How dare they?".

There is one of Derek's stories in which we were asleep after the show in the hotel somewhere in America, and the Mayor's wife comes and says, "Get them up, I want to meet them."

Derek said, "I'm not going to wake them." She started to scream, "You get them up or I'll tell the press." There was always that — they were always threatening that they would tell the press about us, if we didn't see their bloody daughter with her braces on her teeth. It was

always the police chief's daughter or the Lord Mayor's daughter, all the most obnoxious kids — because they had the most obnoxious parents — that we were forced to see all the time. We had these people thrust on us.

The most humiliating experiences were like sitting with the Mayor of the Bahamas, when we were making *Help* and being insulted by these fuckin' junked up middle-class bitches and bastards who would be commenting on our work and commenting on our manners.

I was always drunk, insulting them. I couldn't take it. It would hurt me. I would go insane,

swearing at them. I would do something. I couldn't take it.

All that business was awful, it was a fuckin' humiliation. One has to completely humiliate oneself to be what the Beatles were, and that's what I resent; I didn't know, I didn't foresee. It happened bit by bit, gradually until this complete craziness is surrounding you, and you're doing exactly what you don't want to do with people you can't stand — the people you hated when you were ten.

M.B.E.

John Lennon: We had to do a lot of selling out then. Taking the M.B.E. was a sell-out for me.

You know, before you get an M.B.E. the Palace writes to you to ask if you're going to accept it, because you're not supposed to reject it publicly and they sound you out first.

I chucked the letter in with all the fan-mail, until Brian asked me if I had it. He and a few other people persuaded me that it was in our interests to take it, and it was hypocritical of me to accept it.

But I'm glad, really, that I did accept it — because it meant that four years later I could use it to make a gesture.

We did manage to refuse all sorts of things that people don't know about.

For instance, we did the Royal Variety Show once, and we were asked discreetly to do it every year after that — but we always said "Stuff it".

So every year there was always a story in the newspapers saying: "Why No Beatles For The Queen", which was pretty funny, because they didn't know we'd refused it.

June 11, 1965. H.M. Queen Elizabeth included the Beatles in the birthday honours list, naming them as members of the Most Excellent Order of the British Empire. They were the first rock group to make the honours list. From now on they can use the initials M.B.E. after their names.

What was your reaction when you heard the news?
Ringo: There's a proper medal as well as the letters, isn't there? I will keep it to wear when I'm old. It's the sort of thing you want to keep.
John: I thought you had to drive tanks and win wars to win the M.B.E.
George: I didn't think you got this sort of thing for playing rock 'n' roll music.
Paul: I think it's marvellous. What does this make my dad?

The announcement outraged some existing members of the Order and a few of them returned their medals. One such was Hector Dupuis, a member of the Canadian House of Commons. He claimed that the British royalty had placed him on the "same level as vulgar nincompoops". Dupuis received his medal for his work as director of selective service in Quebec.

What do you say about Dupuis turning in his medal?
George: If Dupuis doesn't want the medal, he had better give it to us. Then we can give it to our manager, Brian Epstein. M.B.E. really stands for 'Mr. Brian Epstein'.
Why do you think you got the medal?
John: I reckon we got it for exports, and the citation should have said that. Look, if someone had got an award for exporting millions of dollars worth of fertilizer or machine tools, everyone would have applauded. So why should they knock us?

The Great Throne Room, Buckingham Palace, October 26, 1965.

The Queen: [*to Paul*] How long have you been together now?
Paul: Oh, for many years.
Ringo: Forty years.
The Queen: [*to Ringo*] Are you the one who started it?
Ringo: No, I was the last to join. I'm the little fellow.
The Queen: [*to John*] Have you been working hard lately?
John: No, we've been on a holiday.

Outside Buckingham Palace four thousand screaming teenagers struggled with police, chanting "Long Live The Queen! Long Live The Beatles!" The Beatles spoke with the press in the courtyard of the palace.

Paul: We've played many palaces including Frisco's Cow Palace. But never this one before. It's a keen pad and I liked the staff. Thought they'd be dukes and things but they were just fellas.
What about the Queen?
Paul: She's lovely, great. She was very friendly. She was just like a mum to us.
Were you nervous?
John: Not as much as some of the other people in there.
How did the other medal recipients act towards your award?
John: One formally-dressed, middle-aged winner walked up to us after the ceremony and said: "I want your autographs for my daughter but I don't know what she sees in you." So we gave him our autographs.
How did you know what to do during the ceremony?
John: This big fellow drilled us. Every time he got to Ringo he kept cracking up.

What will you do with your medals?
Paul: What you normally do with medals. Put them in a box.

John's Books.

How do you write your books?
John: I put things down on sheets of paper and stuff them in my pockets. When I have enough, I have a book.
Why do you kill people off in your books?
John: That's a good way to end them. I suppose they were manifestations of hidden cruelties. They were very Alice in Wonderland and Winnie the Pooh. I was very hung-up then. I got rid of a lot of that. It was my version of what was happening then. It was the usual criticisms as some critic put it.
John, what were you really trying to say in your book? Why don't people understand it?
John: I understand it. If I wrote it in normal spelling there would be no point in writing. I'm not saying anything. There is no message.

John & Jesus.

March 4, 1966. John Lennon was interviewed by Maureen Cleave in the London *Evening Standard*.
John: Christianity will go. It will
vanish and shrink. I needn't argue about that. I'm right and I will be proved right. We're more popular than Jesus now. I don't know which will go first — rock 'n' roll or Christianity. Jesus was all right but his disciples were thick and ordinary. It's them twisting it that ruins it for me.

In the United States, particularly the mid-western Bible Belt, reaction was fast and furious. Radio stations banned the playing of Beatles records and Station KLUE in Longview, Texas, organised a public bonfire of their records. The station manager said, "We are inviting local teenagers to bring in their records and other symbols of the group's popularity to be burned at a public bonfire on Friday night, August 13th."
   The Grand Dragon of the South Carolina Ku Klux Klan attached a Beatles record to a large wooden cross and set the cross on fire during a ceremony.
   The Rev. Thurman H. Babbs, pastor of the New Haven Baptist Church in Cleveland, Ohio, said, "I will revoke the membership of any member of my church who agrees with John Lennon's remarks about Jesus or who goes to see the Beatles."

John: I'm not anti-God, anti-Christ or anti-religion. I was not saying we are greater or better. I believe in God, but not as one thing, not as an old man in the sky. I believe that what

people call God is something in all of us. I believe that what Jesus and Mohammed and Buddha and all the rest said was right. It's just that the translations have gone wrong. I wasn't saying the Beatles are better than God or Jesus. I used *Beatles* because it's easy for me to talk about Beatles. I could have said TV or the cinema or anything popular and I would have gotten away with it.

Are you sorry about your statement concerning Christ?
John: I wasn't saying whatever they're saying I was saying. . . . I'm sorry I said it, really. I never meant it to be a lousy anti-religious thing. From what I've read, or observed, Christianity just seems to me to be shrinking, to be losing contact. My views on Christianity are directly influenced by a book, *The Passover Plot*, by Hugh J. Schonfield. The premise in it is that Jesus' message had been garbled by his disciples and twisted for a variety of self-serving reasons by those who followed, to the point where it has lost validity for many in the modern age . . . The passage which caused all the trouble was part of a long profile Maureen Cleave was doing for the London *Evening Standard* . . . Then, the mere fact that it was in *Datebook* changed its meaning that much more.
What was your own formal religious background?
John: Normal Church of England, Sunday School and Sunday Church. But there was actually nothing going on in the church I went to. Nothing really touched us.
How about when you got older?
John: By the time I was 19, I was cynical about religion and never even considered about the goings on in Christianity. It's only in the last two years I — all the Beatles — have started looking for something else. We live in a moving hothouse. We've been mushroom-grown, forced to grow up a bit quick, like having 30-to-40-year-old heads in 20-year-old bodies. We had to develop more sides, more attitudes. If you're a bus man, you usually have a bus man's attitude. But we had to sort of be more than four mopheads up on a stage. We had to grow up or we'd have been swamped.
Why did you subject yourself to a public apology in front of television cameras?
John: If I were at the stage I was five years ago, I would have shouted we'd never tour again and packed myself off and that would be the end of it. Lord knows I don't need the money. But the record burning. That was a real shock, the physical burning. I couldn't go away knowing that I created another little place of hate in the world. Especially with something as uncomplicated as people listening to records and dancing and playing and enjoying what the Beatles are. Not when I could do something

about it. If I say tomorrow I'm not going to play again, I still couldn't live in a place with somebody hating me for something irrational.
Why don't you tell your fans all this?
John: But that's the trouble with being truthful. You try to apply truth talk, although you have to be false sometimes because the whole thing is false in a way, like a game. But you hope sometime that if you're truthful with somebody, they'll stop all the plastic reaction and be truthful back and it'll be worth it. But everybody is playing the game and sometimes I'm left naked and truthful with everybody biting me. It's disappointing.

Radio station KLUE, the station which organised the public bonfire of Beatles records on August 13th, was knocked off the air the next morning when a bolt of lightning struck their transmission tower, knocking their news director unconscious and causing extensive damage to their radio equipment.

Brian Epstein's Death.

John Lennon: After Brian died, we collapsed. Paul took over and supposedly led us. But what is leading us, when we went round in circles? We broke up then. That was the disintegration.

I just did it like a job. The Beatles broke up after Brian died; we made the double album, the set. It's like if you took each track off it and made it all mine and all George's. It's like I told you many times, it was just me and a backing group, Paul and a backing group, and I enjoyed it. We broke up then.

We were in Wales with the Maharishi. We had just gone down after seeing his lecture first night. We heard it then, and then we went right off into the Maharishi thing.

We were just outside a lecture hall with Maharishi and I don't know... I can't remember, it just sort of came over. Somebody came up to us ... the press were there, because we had gone down with this strange Indian, and they said, "Brian's dead" and I was stunned, we all were, I suppose, and the Maharishi, we went in to him. "What, he's dead," and all that, and he was sort of saying oh, forget it, be happy, like an idiot, like parents, smile, that's what the Maharishi said. And we did.

I knew that we were in trouble then. I didn't really have any misconceptions about our ability to do anything other than play music and I was scared. I thought, we've fuckin' had it.

I liked Brian and I had a very close relationship with him for years, like I have with Allen [Klein] because I'm not gonna have some stranger runnin' things, that's all. I like to work with friends. I was the closest with Brian, as close as you can get to somebody who lives a sort of "fag" life, and you don't really know what

they're doin' on the side. But in the group, I was closest to him and I did like him.

He had great qualities and he was good fun. He had a flair. He was a theatrical man, rather than a businessman. When he got Cilla Black, his great delight was to dress her and present her. He would have made a great dress designer, 'cause that's what he was made for. With us he was a bit like that. I mean, he literally fuckin' cleaned us up and there were great fights between him and me over me not wanting to dress up. In fact, he and Paul had some kind of collusion to keep me straight because I kept spoilin' the image.

We had complete faith in him when he was runnin' us. To us, he was the expert. I mean originally he had a shop. Anybody who's got a shop must be all right. He went around smarmin' and charmin' everybody. He had hellish tempers and fits and lock-outs and y'know he'd vanish for days. He'd come to a crisis every now and then and the whole business would fuckin' stop 'cause he'd be on sleepin' pills for days on end and wouldn't wake up. Or he'd be missin' y'know, beaten up by some docker down the Old Kent Road. But we weren't too aware of it. It was later on we started findin' out about those things.

We'd never have made it without him and *vice versa.* Brian contributed as much as us in the early days, although we were the talent and he was the hustler. He wasn't strong enough to overbear us. Brian could never make us do what we really didn't want to do.

The Maharishi.

Ringo: The four of us have had the most hectic lives. We have got almost anything money can buy. But when you can do that, the things you buy mean nothing after a time. You look for something else, for a new experience. It's like your Dad going to the boozer and you want to find out what the taste of drink is like. We have found something now which fills the gap. Since meeting His Holiness, Maharishi Mahesh Yogi, I feel great.
Paul: I now realize that taking drugs was like taking an aspirin without having a headache.
John: If we'd met Maharishi before we had taken LSD, we wouldn't have needed to take it.
George: We haven't really started yet. We've only just discovered what we can do as musicians, what thresholds we can cross. The future stretches out beyond our imagination.
John: Bangor was incredible, you know. Maharishi reckons the message will get through if we can put it across. What he says about life and the universe is the same message that Jesus, Buddha and Krishna and all the big boys were putting over. Mick came up there and he got a

sniff and he was on the phone saying: "Send Keith, send Brian, send them all down. You just get a sniff and you're hooked."

George: But with meditation you don't have to bother with religion or anything. When you come out after meditating in the morning, you forget it completely and let it work for you.

John: Yeh, and there's none of this sitting in the lotus position or standing on your head. You just do it as long as you like. [*In a heavy accent*] Twenty minutes a day is prescribed for ze verkers. Twenty minutes in the morning and tventy minutes after verk. Makes you happy, intelligent and more energy. I mean look how it all started. I believe he just landed in Hawaii in his nightshirt, all on his own, nobody with him, in 1958.

George: It helps you find fulfilment in life, helps you live life to the full. Young people are searching for a bit of peace inside themselves.

John: The main thing is not to think about the future or the past, the main thing is just to get on with *now*. We want to help people do that with these academies. We'll make a donation and we'll ask for money from anyone we know with money, anyone that's interested, anyone in the so-called establishment who's worried about kids going wild and drugs and all that. Another groovy thing: everybody gives one week's wages when they join. I think it's the fairest thing I've ever heard of. And that's all you ever pay, just the once.

George: Patti started it all really.

Patti: A girl friend told me about it and I'd been going several months.

John: I didn't believe it at the time. She said: "They gave me this word but I can't tell you, it's a secret." And I said: "What kind of scene is this if you keep secrets from your friends?"

George: She joined the Maharishi place a long time ago. We'd been looking for this thing and suddenly it's there. First of all it was the Indian music and when I was in India I was lucky enough to meet Ravi Shankar.

John: With Brian dying it was sort of a big thing for us. And if we hadn't had this meditation it would have been much harder to assess and carry on and know how we were going.

Now we're our managers, now we have to make all the decisions. We've always had full responsibility for what we did, but we still had a father figure, or whatever it was, and if we didn't feel like it — well, you know, Brian would do it. Now we've got to work out all our business, everything, and maybe a lot more to do with NEMS and all the things that Brian left behind. It threw me quite a bit. But then the Maharishi talked to us and, I don't know, cooled us out a bit.

George: We've all come along the same path. We've been together a long time. We learned

right from the beginning that we're going to be together.

John: Even if you go into the meditation bit just curious or cynical, once you go into it, you see. We weren't so much sceptical because we'd been through that phase in the middle of all the Beatlemania like, so we came out of being sceptics a bit. But you've still got to have a questioning attitude to all that goes on. The only thing you can do is judge on your own experience and that's what this is about. You know, I'm less sceptical than I ever was.

George: We don't know how this will come out in the music. Don't expect to hear transcendental meditation all the time.

John: I don't honestly know how anything I've felt has come out in my music, it's usually in retrospect I've seen what I've been saying.

George: It'll take us time. You see we don't want this thing to come out like Cliff and Billy Graham. You know how that just comes out and then it's finished straight away. We mean it.

John: Well, so does Cliff.

George: Right. I'd rather not use any obvious things until you can see how it's naturally affected the music.

John: The same as we didn't really shove our LP full of pot and drugs, but I mean there was an effect. You were more consciously trying to keep it out. You wouldn't say: "I had some acid, baby, so groovy," but there was a sort of feeling that something happened between *Revolver* and *Sgt. Pepper*. I mean, whether it would have happened anyway is speculation.

George: Well, when I went to San Francisco this was great. This was the first thing that turned me off drugs. Seeing the Haight-Ashbury.

John: We'd dropped drugs before this meditation thing. George mentioned he was dropping out of it and I said: "Well, it's not doing me any harm, I'll carry on." But I just suddenly thought, I've seen all that scene. There's no point and if it does do anything to your chemistry or brains? Then someone wrote to me and said that whether you like it or not, whether you have no ill-effects, something happens up there. So I decided if I ever did meet someone who could tell me the answer, I'd have nothing left to do it with.

George: There's still the craze. Usually the people who establish something that becomes a craze, well, they're usually very sincere people. It's just when they all the publicity comes, then it turns bad. The thing that happened with this movement, the hippy thing, is that in Haight-Ashbury . . .

John [*interrupting*]: It couldn't make it with a name like Haight-Ashbury.

George: People who live in America and live round there, they told me that most of the original people that came in there with the love

and flower thing, well, they've cleared out into the country. They're just living in communities of farms or tents.

When I was there I expected something like the King's Road, only more. Somehow I expected them all to own their own little shops because I'd heard they've all bought out blocks. I expected them all to be nice and clean and friendly and happy. And then the first thing you see is just lots of dirty people just lying round the floor. Which just puts you off for a start. With the hippies there's the good side and the bad side. There were so many nice people that I saw. It was obvious, you can see people who just vibrate a little happiness. And then there's the other sick part of it where you see people so out of their minds with drugs and who really believe the drug's the thing that's doing it. That's the sad bit and that overpowered the good bit for me.

And that was the thing. Right there and then. It was the identification with all those druggies — if you want to call them that, I call them that — because they're the people. It's different if somebody takes a drug for things or even for kicks, but when they start believing in the drug...

John [*interrupting*]: Worshipping it.

George: Then it's wrong. With this thing of us becoming so related to the hippies, that's why it's so important.

John: There's a big academy of this meditation scene out in California and if even just two hundred of them try it, just because of what we say, they'll turn the next two hundred on themselves as soon as they've done it, and that might have been worth all the Haight-Ashbury and all the drop-outs. The point about how the English are taking it now seems to me to be better. It's not drop out, it's drop in and change it.

George: It's drop out of the old established way of thought, the narrow concept of life. To act and try to make as many changes as possible — this is the thing, to drop in with this changed concept of life and try to influence as many people.

John: You know, I feel I can handle anything at the moment and I never felt like that before. You know, I've had good days, bad days, periods when things are going right, but I mean this is a bad period for us in the material sense, in the physical sense. But the greatest period in an inner sense.

John wrote 'Sexie Sadie' about the Maharishi.

John: That's about the Maharishi, yes. I copped out and I wouldn't write "Maharishi what have you done, you made a fool of everyone". But, now it can be told, Fab Listeners. I just sort of *saw* him. There was a big hullaballo about him trying to rape Mia Farrow or somebody and trying to get off with a few other women and things like that. We went to see him, after we stayed up all night discussing was it true or not

PATTI BOYD

true. When George started thinking it might be true, I thought well, it must be true; because if George started thinking it might be true, there must be something in it.

So we went to see Maharishi, the whole gang of us, the next day, charged down to his hut, his

bungalow, his very rich-looking bungalow in the mountains, and as usual, when the dirty work came, I was the spokesman — whenever the dirty work came, I actually had to be leader, wherever the scene was, when it came to the nitty gritty, I had to do the speaking — and I said

"We're leaving."

"Why?" he asked, and all that shit and I said, "Well, if you're so *cosmic*, you'll know why."

He was always intimating, and there were all these right hand men always intimating, that he did miracles. And I said, "You know why," and he said, "I don't know why, you must tell me," and I just kept saying "You ought to know" and he gave me a look like, "I'll kill you, you bastard," and he gave me such a look. I knew then. I had called his bluff and I was bit rough to him.

Yoko: You expected too much from him.

John: I always do, I always expect too much. I was always expecting my mother and never got her. That's what it is, you know, or some parent, I know that much.

John: No ethnic bastard's gonna get no golden castles outta me!

Apple.

Paul McCartney: We want to help other people, but without doing it like charity and without seeming like patrons of the arts. *We* always had to go to the big man on our knees, touch our forelocks and say, "Please, can we do so and so?" And most of those companies are so big, and so out of touch with people like us who just want to sing or make films, that everyone has a bad time. We are just trying to set up a good organisation, not some great fat institution that doesn't care. We don't want people to say yessir nossir. We hope that at Apple if someone can produce a record better than me they'll say so: I'm not on some big ego-trip. I mean, we're in the happy position of not needing any more money, so for the first time the bosses aren't in it for the profit. If you come to see me and say "I've had such-and-such a dream," I will say "Here's so much money. Go away and do it."

We've already bought all *our* dreams. We want to share that possibility with others. When we were touring, and when the adoration and hysteria were at a peak, if we'd been the shrewd operators we were often made out to be, we might have thought — *that's* nice! Ah. Click. Let's use this for our own evil ends. But there's no desire in any of our heads to take over the world. That was Hitler. That's what he wanted to do. There is, however, a desire to get power in order to use it for good.

John Lennon: The aim of the company isn't a stack of gold teeth in the bank. We've done that bit. It's more of a trick to see if we can get artistic freedom within a business structure; to see if we can create things and sell them without charging three times our cost.

What happened at Apple?
John: Apple was a manifestation of Beatle naivety, collective naivety. We said, "We're going to do this and help everybody" and all that and we got conned on the subtlest and bluntest level. We really didn't get approached by the best artists, we got all the bums from everywhere else. All the ones that everyone had thrown out. The ones who were really groovy wouldn't approach us because they were too proud.
Or maybe they don't like hustling.
John: Right, 'cause I don't like hustling. I couldn't do it!
The only way to reach you people is to hustle.
John: Right, and that's why it didn't work.

We had to quickly build up another wall round us to protect us from all the beggars and lepers in Britain and America who came to see us. Our lives were getting insane! I tried when we were in Wigmore Street [*Apple's original offices*], to see everyone like we said, everyone day in and day out, and there wasn't anyone who had anything to offer to society or me or anything. There was just, "I want, I want, and why not?" and terrible scenes like that going on in the offices with different spades and hippies and all different people very wild with me. Even on the peace campaign we had a lot of that too. Once you open the door it's hard you know.

What's the answer? You obviously don't want to close yourself off.

John: I just have to take it slower and I have to deal with people, even people who are thinking the same way as us, and we have to agree on steps to be taken. Make a deal, whether it's on paper or a shake of the hand and then move forward together. At a bit slower pace. See, I'm very impetuous, so I like it NOW, everything tomorrow, and I'm beginning to find out it doesn't work. It's just impossible to do it like that so I've got to slow down. All the money went into a box and never came out so nobody got it. Apple as it is now is all right, obviously by the charts and everything.

Does the track 'You Never Give Me Your Money' relate to that?

John [*laughs*]: Well I don't know, that's Paul you know, I think it's something to do with what Paul's thinking at the moment, you know, "Give me your funny paper" — but it seems to be coming true!

People were robbing us and living on us to the tune of . . . 18 or 20 thousand pounds a week, was rolling out of Apple and nobody was doing anything about it. All our buddies that worked for us for fifty years, were all just living and drinking and eating like fuckin' Rome, and I suddenly realized it and said we're losing money at such a rate that we would have been broke, really broke. We didn't have anything in the bank really, none of us did. Paul and I could have probably floated, but we were sinking fast. It was just hell, and it had to stop.

The Break-up.

John Lennon: I said to Paul, "I'm leaving". I knew on the flight over to Toronto or before we went to Toronto: I told Allen I was leaving, I told Eric Clapton and Klaus that I was leaving then, but that I would probably like to use them as a group. I hadn't decided how to do it — to have a permanent new group or what — then later on, I thought fuck, I'm not going to get stuck with another set of people, whoever they are.

I announced it to myself and the people around me on the way to Toronto a few days before. And on the plane — Klein came with me — I told Allen, "It's over". When I got back, there were a few meetings, and Allen said well, cool it, cool it, there was a lot to do, business-

PAUL McCARTNEY AND MARY HOPKIN

wise you know, and it would not have been suitable at the time.

Then we were discussing something in the office with Paul, and Paul said something or other about the Beatles doing something, and I kept saying "No, no, no," to everything he said. So it came to a point where I had to say something, of course, and Paul said, "What do you mean?"

I said, "I mean the group is over, I'm leaving."

Allen was there, and he will remember exactly and Yoko will, but this is exactly how I see it. Allen was saying don't tell. He didn't want me to tell Paul even. So I said, "It's out." I couldn't stop it, it came out. Paul and Allen both said that they were glad that I wasn't going to announce it, that I wasn't going to make an event out of it. I don't know whether Paul said don't tell anybody, but he was darned pleased that I wasn't going to. He said, "Oh, that means nothing really happened if you're not going to say anything."

So that's what happened. So, like anybody when you say divorce, their face goes all sorts of colours. It's like he knew really that this was the final thing; and six months later he comes out with whatever. I was a fool not to do it, not to do what Paul did, which was use it to sell a record. **Paul McCartney:** The real break-up in the

Beatles was months ago. First Ringo left when we were doing the "White Album", because he said he didn't think it was any fun playing with us any more. But after two days of us telling him he was the greatest drummer in the world for the Beatles — which I believe — he came back. Then George left when we were making *Abbey Road*, because he didn't think he had enough say in our records — which was fair enough. After a couple of days he came back.

And then last autumn I began to feel that the only way we could ever get back to the stage of playing good music again was to start behaving as a band again. But I didn't want to go out and face 200,000 — because I would get nothing from it, so I thought up this idea of playing surprise one-night stands in unlikely places — just letting 100 people in the village hall, so to speak, and then locking the doors. It would have been a great scene for those who saw us, and for us, too.

So one day when we had a meeting I told the others about my idea, and asked them what they thought of it. John said, "I think you're daft." I said, "What do you mean?" I mean he is John Lennon, and I'm a bit scared of all that rapier wit we hear about. And he just said "I think you're daft. I'm leaving the Beatles. I want a divorce."

Press Conferences.

Beethoven figures in one of your songs.
What do you think of Beethoven?
Ringo: He's great. Especially his poetry.

Do you believe in lunacy?
Ringo: Yeah; it's healthy.
But aren't you embarrassed by all the lunacy?
Ringo: No, it's crazy.

Ringo, why do you wear two rings on each hand?
Ringo: Because I can't fit them through my nose.

What do you think of Christine Keeler?
Ringo: She's a great comic.

Do you think it's wrong to set such a bad example to teenagers, smoking the way you do?
Ringo: It's better than being alcoholics.

What do you think of the criticism that you are not very good?
George: We're not.

What do you believe is the reason you are the most popular singing group today?
John: We've no idea. If we did, we'd get four long-haired boys, put them together and become their managers.

You've admitted to being agnostics. Are you also irreverent?
Paul: We are agnostics so there is no point in being irreverent.

What did you think when your airliner's engine began smoking as you landed today?
Ringo: Beatles, women and children first!

Paul: Nothing annoys us really. Some things make us laugh. Like those stamp out the Beatles gags. And the other day a photographer asked if he could take two pictures of us. One with our wigs on and one with our wigs off.

Why do teenagers stand up and scream piercingly and painfully when you appear?
Paul: None of us know. But we've heard that teenagers go to our shows just to scream. A lot of them don't even want to listen because they have

our records. We kind of like the screaming teenagers. If they want to pay their money and sit out there and shout, that's their business. We aren't going to be like little dictators and say "You've got to shut up". The commotion doesn't bother us anymore. It's come to be like working in a bell factory. You don't hear the bells after a while.

What is your personal goal?
George: To do as well as I can at whatever I attempt. And someday to die with a peaceful mind.
But you really don't expect that to happen for a long time yet, do you?
George: When your number's up, it's up.

Do you plan to marry Jane Asher?
Paul: I've got no plans. But everybody keeps saying I have. Maybe they know better. They say I'm married and divorced and have fifty kids so you might as well too.

What kind of music do you like?
Paul: Coloured American groups.

What started your practice of wearing four rings at once?
Ringo: Six got to be too heavy.

Why do you think you get more fan mail than anyone else in the group?
Ringo: I dunno. I suppose it's because more people write me.

Do you date much?
Ringo: What are you doing tonight?

Do you fight amongst yourselves?
John: Only in the mornings.

What do you miss most now that your fame prohibits your freedom?
Ringo: Going to the movies.
George: Having nothing to do.
John: School, because you don't have much to do there.
Paul: Going on buses.

What impresses you most about America?
John: Bread.
Paul: Going on buses.

On arriving in USA...

How do you like this welcome?
Ringo: So this is America. They all seem out of their minds.

What do you do when you're cooped up in a hotel room between shows?
George: We ice skate.

Why are your speaking voices different from your singing voices?
George: We don't have a musical background.

Do you like fish and chips?
Ringo: Yes, but I like steak and chips better.

How tall are you?
Ringo: Two feet, nine inches.

Paul, what do you think of columnist Walter Winchell?
Paul: He said I'm married and I'm not.
George: Maybe he wants to marry you?

How did you find America?
Ringo: We went to Greenland and made a left turn.

Would you like to walk down the street without being recognised?
John: We used to do this with no money in our pockets. There's no point in it.

Where would you like to go if all the security wasn't necessary?
John: Harlem.

Are you scared when crowds scream at you?
John: More so in Dallas than in other places perhaps.

How do you feel about other Beatle-type groups?
John: The Rolling Stones are personal friends of ours. They are most creative and beginning to write good songs.

Is it true you can't sing?
John [*points to George*]: Not me. Him.

Do you like being Beatles?
John: Yes, or we'd be the Rolling Stones.

Why don't you smile, George?
George: I'll hurt my lips.

Do you plan to record any anti-war songs?
John: All our songs are anti-war.

What's your reaction to a Seattle psychiatrist's opinion that you are a menace?
George: Psychiatrists are a menace.

When you do a new song, how do you decide who sings the lead?
John: We just get together and whoever knows most of the words sings the lead.

What's this about an annual illness, George?
George: I get cancer every year.

How do you keep your psychic balance?
Ringo: The important thing is not to get potty. There's four of us so, whenever one of us gets a little potty the other three bring him back to earth.

What do you think you've contributed to the musical field?
Ringo: Records.
George: A laugh and a smile.

How does it feel putting on the whole world?
Ringo: We enjoy it.
Paul: We aren't really putting you on.
George: Just a bit of it.
John: How does it feel to be put on?

Does all the adulation from teenage girls affect you?
John: When I feel my head start to swell, I look at Ringo and know perfectly well we're not supermen.

What's your reaction to composer Aaron Copland who found the Beatles music interesting and Richard Rodgers who found it boring?
Paul: I like anyone who says he likes our music. I don't mind Richard Rodgers saying he finds it boring — but I must add that I find Richard Rodgers' music boring. And I'm not being nasty, Richard.

How do you feel about a night club, Arthur, named after your hairstyle?
George: I was proud — until I saw the night club.

What do you consider the most important thing in life?
George: Love.

Do you resent fans ripping up your sheets for souvenirs?
Ringo: No I don't mind. So long as I'm not in them while the ripping is going on.

Paul: I once knew a fellow on the Dingle who had two dads. He used to call them number one dad and number two dad. Now apparently number one dad wasn't nice. He used to throw the boy on the fire — which can develop a lot of complexes in a young lad.
Ringo: I remember my uncle putting the red-hot poker on me, and that's no lie. He was trying to frighten me.
Paul: Tell me, Ringo, do all your relatives go around applying red-hot pokers to you?
John: It's the only way they can identify them.
Paul: You see, Ringo comes from a depressed area.
John: Some people call it the slums.
Ringo: No, the slums are farther.

Paul: At school we had a great hip English master and instead of keeping us to the drag stuff like *Return Of The Native* he would let us read Tennessee Williams and *Lady Chatterley's Lover* and *The Miller's Tale*.

John: I get spasms of being intellectual. I read a bit about politics but I don't think I'd vote for anyone. No message from any of those phoney politicians is coming through to me.

George: We've always had laughs. Sometimes we find ourselves hysterical, especially when we're tired. We laugh at soft remarks that the majority of people don't get.

John: The thing I'm afraid of is growing old. I hate that. You get old and you've missed it somehow. The old always resent the young and *vice versa*.

Ringo: I'd like to end up sort of unforgettable.

John: Ours is a today image.

What's the most unusual request you've had?
John: I wouldn't like to say.

Ringo: I don't like talking. It's how I'm built. Some people gab all day and some people play it smogo. I don't mind talking or smiling. It's just, I don't do it very much. I haven't got a smiling face or a talking mouth.

John: We're not going to fizzle out in half a day. But afterwards I'm not going to change into a tap dancing musical. I'll just develop what I'm doing at the moment, although whatever I say now I'll change my mind next week. I mean, we all know that bit about "It won't be the same when you're twenty-five". I couldn't care less. This isn't show business. It's something else. This is different from anything that anybody imagines. You don't go on from this. You do this and then you finish.

At the Royal Command Variety Performance at the Prince of Wales Theatre in Piccadilly Circus with the Queen Mother and Princess Margaret present . . .

John: On this next number I want you all to join in. Would those in the cheap seats clap their hands. The rest of you can rattle your jewellery.

Afterwards the Beatles were presented to the Queen Mother. She asked them where they would be performing next. At Slough, they told her. "Ah," she said with delight, "that's near us."

BBC: *How important is it to succeed here [in Paris]?*
Paul: It is important to succeed everywhere.
BBC: *The French have not made up their minds about the Beatles. What do you think of them?*
John: Oh, we like the Beatles. They're gear.

Do you like topless bathing suits?
Ringo: We've been wearing them for years.
Why don't you like Donald Duck?
Ringo: I could never understand him.

Girls rushed toward my car because it had press identification and they thought I met you. How do you explain this phenomenon?
John: You're lovely to look at.

How do you stand in the draft?
John: About five feet, eleven inches.

What about your future?
John: It looks nice.

Ringo: None of us has quite grasped what it is all about yet. It's washing over our heads like a huge tidal wave. But we're young. Youth is on our side. And it's youth that matters right now. I don't care about politics, *just people.*

George: I wouldn't do all this if I didn't like it. I wouldn't do anything I didn't want to, would I?

Paul: Security is the only thing I want. Money to do nothing with, money to have in case you wanted to do something.

John: People say we're loaded with money but by comparison with those who are supposed to talk the Queen's English that's ridiculous. We're only earning. They've got capital behind them and they're earning on top of that. The more people you meet, the more you realize it's all a class thing.

John: No more unscheduled public appearances. We've had enough. We're going to stay in our hotel except for concerts.
Won't this make you feel like caged animals?
John: No. We feed ourselves.

What did you think of Miami?
Ringo: The sun. I didn't know what it meant until I got there. But I am breathtaken to be back in England.

Were you worried about the oversized roughnecks who tried to infiltrate the airport crowd on your arrival?
Ringo: That was us.

How do you add up success?
John, Paul, George, Ringo: Money.

What will you do when Beatlemania subsides?
John: Count the money.

John: I don't suppose I think much about the future. I don't really give a damn. Though now we've made it, it would be a pity to get bombed. It's selfish but I don't care too much about humanity — I'm an escapist. Everybody's always drumming on about the future but I'm not letting it interfere with my laughs, if you see what I mean. Perhaps I was worried more when I was working it out about God.

George: Naturally I'm part of my generation. I like the way people bring things out into the open. I'd hate it if when you spoke about sex everybody curled away.

Paul: It's disturbing that people should go around blowing us up, but if an atom bomb should explode I'd say, "Oh well", No point in saying anything else, is there? People are so crackers. I know the bomb is ethically wrong but I won't go around crying. I suppose I could do something like wearing those 'ban the bomb' things, but it's something like religion that I don't think about. It doesn't fit in with my life.

Paul: Don't for heavens sake say we're the new youth, because that's a load of old rubbish.

Are you ever in any danger during your concerts?
Paul: I was got once by a cigarette lighter. Clouted me right in the eye and closed my eye for the stay. In Chicago a purple and yellow stuffed animal, a red rubber ball and a skipping rope were plopped up on stage. I had to kick a carton of Winston cigarettes out of the way when I played. And I saw a cigarette lighter go flying past me in Detroit's Olympia Stadium.
Don't you worry about all that?
Paul: It's okay, as long as they throw the light stuff, like paper.

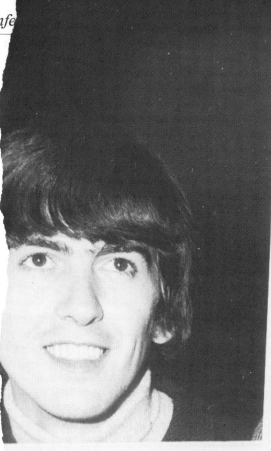

Brian Epstein: That was quite a nice aircraft we flew back on.
Ringo: Let's buy it!

Do you care what the public thinks about your private lives?
Ringo: There's a woman in the United States who predicted the plane we were travelling on would crash. Now a lot of people would like to think we were scared into saying a prayer. What we did actually — we drank.

What do you think of space shots?
John: You see one, you've seen them all.

What do you think about the pamphlet calling you four Communists?
Paul: Us, Communists? Why we can't be Communists. We're the world's number one capitalists. Imagine us, Communists!

Would you ever accept a girl in your group if she could sing, play an instrument and wear the Beatle haircut?
Ringo: How tall is she?

What about the recent criticism of your lyrics?
Paul: If you start reading things into them you might as well start singing hymns.

Beatle-licensed products have grossed millions and millions of dollars in America alone — Beatle wigs, Beatle hats, Beatle T-shirts, Beatle egg-cups, Beatlenut ice-cream...
Ringo: Anytime you spell Beatle with an "a" in it, we get some money.

What are your favourite programmes on American television?
Paul: 'News In Espanol' from Miami. Popeye, Bullwinkle. All the cultural stuff.
John: I like American TV because you can get eighteen stations, but you can't get a good picture on any one of them.

You were at the Playboy Club last night. What did you think of it?
Paul: The Playboy and I are just good friends.

George, is the place you were brought up a bit like Greenwich Village?
George: No. More like The Bowery.

Ringo, how do you manage to find all those parties?
Ringo: I don't know. I just end up at them.
Paul: On tour we don't go out much. Ringo's always out though.
John: Ringo freelances.

There's a 'Stamp Out The Beatles' movement underway in Detroit. What are you going to do about it?
Paul: We're going to start a campaign to stamp out Detroit.

Who thought up the name, Beatles?
Paul: I thought of it.
Why?
Paul: Why not?

Aren't you tired of all the hocus-pocus? Wouldn't you rather sit on your fat wallets?
Paul: When we get tired we take fat vacations on our fat wallets.

Do you get much fan mail?
Ringo: We get 2,000 letters a day.
John: We're going to answer every one of them.

Do any of you have ulcers?
George: None that we've noticed.

How come you were turned back by immigration?
John: We had to be deloused.

What is your favourite food?
Ringo: I'm hung up on hamburgers.
George: All four of us are mad about hero sandwiches.
Paul: I have a yen for grilled cheese sandwiches.
John: George and I usually wait until someone else orders, then say, "I'll have that too".

How do you feel about the invasion of your privacy all the time?
Ringo: The only time it bothers us is when they get us to the floor and really mangle us.

Do you worry about smoking in public? Do you think it might set a bad example for your younger fans?
George: We don't set examples. We smoke because we've always smoked. Kids don't smoke because we do. They smoke because they want to. If we changed we'd be putting on an act.
Ringo: [whispering] We even drink.

What careers would you individually have chosen had you not become entertainers?
Ringo: A hairdresser.
George: I had a short go at being an electrician's apprentice, but I kept blowing things up so I got dumped.
Paul: I dunno. Maybe something with art in it?
John: No comment.

Who in the world would the Beatles like to meet more than anyone else?
Ringo: The real Santa Claus.

Paul, you look like my son.
Paul: You don't look a bit like my mother.

Why aren't you wearing a hat?
George: Why aren't you wearing a tie?

Is it true that on one flight the stewardess broke up a pillow fight among you guys and got clobbered on the head?
George: I'm not really sure where she got hit. She did make us break it up though.

George: Remember that house we stayed in at Harlech?
Paul: No. Which one?
George: Yes you do! There was a woman who had a dog with no legs. She used to take it out in the morning for a slide.

Do teenagers scream at you because they are, in effect, revolting against their parents?
Paul: They've been revolting for years.
John: I've never noticed them revolting.

Do you have any special messages for the Prime Minister and your parents?
John: Hello, Alec.
George: Hello, Muddah.
Ringo: Hello, fellas.

Do you have any special message for Dutch youth?
John: Tell them to buy Beatle records.

Are you afraid military service might break up your careers?
John: No. There's no draft in England now. We're going to let you do our fighting for us.

Is your popularity beginning to taper off?
Paul: I agree that our popularity has hit a peak. But I also agreed with a man who said the same thing last year. And we were both wrong.

Do you speak French?
Paul: Non.

What's the secret of your success?
John: We have a press agent.

Is it true none of you can read and write music?
Paul: None of us can read or write music. The way we work is like, we just whistle. John will whistle at me and I'll whistle back at him.

Do you have any special advice for teenagers?
John: Don't get pimples.

How do you manage to have such a weird effect over teenagers?
George: Enthusiasm, I guess.

Did you really use four letter words on the tourists in the Bahamas?
John: What we actually said was "Gosh".
Paul: We may have also said "Heavens!"
John: Couldn't have said that, Paul. More than four letters.

Sorry to interrupt you while you are eating but what do you think you will be doing in five years time when all this is over?
Ringo: Still eating.

What would you do if the fans got past the police lines?
George: We'd die laughing.

How long will your popularity last?
John: When you're going to go, you're going to go.

What will you do when the bubble bursts?
George: Take up icehockey.
Paul: Play basketball.

H.R.H. Prince Philip presented the awards for "The Most Outstanding Beat Group Of The Year" and "The Most Outstanding Vocal Group Of The Year" to the Beatles.
Prince Philip: Which one of you wrote the book?
John: [raising his hand] Me, Sir.
Prince Philip: I'll swap you one of mine for one of yours.
John: Sure!
Prince Philip: You don't know what you are letting yourself in for.

How do you feel about band leader Ray Block's statement that the Beatles won't last a year?
John: We'll probably last longer than Ray Block.

How come the Beatles, rather than 200 other groups, clicked?
Ringo: Sometimes I try to figure that out too.

Why don't all four of the Beatles ever sing together?
George: Well, we try to start out together anyway.

What does each Beatle consider his two most valued possessions?
John: Our lives.

What do you do with your money?
Ringo: We bury it.
George: We hide it.
Paul: We don't see it. It goes to our office.
John: We pay a lot of taxes.

What are your feelings on the "hints of queerness" American males found in the Beatles during the early days of your climb to popularity?
Paul: There's more terror of that hint of queerness — of homosexuality — here than in England where long hair is more accepted. Our whole promotion made us look silly. But we've had a chance to talk to people since then and they can see we're not thick little kids.

Has success spoiled the Beatles?
John: Well, you don't see us running out and buying bowler hats, do you? I think we've pretty well succeeded in remaining ourselves.
Paul: The great thing about it is that you don't have big worries anymore when you've got where we have — only little ones, like whether the plane is going to crash.

What is it like being the Beatles?
George: We've gotten to know each other quite well. We can stand each other better now than when we first met.

What do you plan to do after this?
Ringo: What else is there to do?

Hair.

What excuse do you have for your collar-length hair?
John: Well, it just grows out yer head.

Which of you is really bald?
George: We're all bald. And I'm deaf and dumb.

Do you ever think of getting a haircut?
George: No, luv, do you?

Where did you think up the hairdos?
Paul: We got them from a German photographer who wore his hair this way.
George: It was while we were in Germany. I went in swimming and when I came out I didn't have a comb. So my hair just dried. The others liked it the way it looked and there we were.
John: We've told so many lies about it we've forgotten.

Do you wear wigs?
John: If we do they must be the only ones with real dandruff.

How do you feel about teenagers imitating you with Beatle wigs?
John: They're not imitating us because we don't wear Beatle wigs.

Where did you get your hair style?
Paul: From Napoleon. And Julius Caesar too. We cut it anytime we feel like it.
Ringo: We may do it now.

Are you wearing wigs or real hair?
Ringo: Hey, where's the police?
Paul: Take her out!
George: Our hair's real. What about yours, lady?

What would happen if you all switched to crewcuts?
John: It would probably be the end of the act.

Are you going to get haircuts over in America?
Ringo: What d'you mean? We got them yesterday.

Does your hair require any special attention?
John: Inattention is the main thing.

What do you look like with your hair back on your foreheads?
John: You just don't do that, mate. You feel naked if you do that, like you don't have any trousers on.

Don't you feel icky and dirty with your hair so long, flopping in your eyes and down your neck?
John: Of course not. We've got combs you know.

What is the biggest threat to your careers, the atom bomb or dandruff?
Ringo: The atom bomb. We've already got dandruff.

Songwriting.

Paul McCartney: Well, first, I started off on my own. Very early on I met John, and we then, gradually, started to write stuff together. Which didn't mean we wrote everything together. We'd kind of write 80% together and the other 20% for me were things like 'Yesterday' and for John things like 'Strawberry Fields' that he'd mainly write on his own. And I did certain stuff on my own. So I've done stuff on my own.

When I first started writing songs I started using a guitar. The first one I ever wrote was one called 'My Little Girl' which is a funny little song, a nice little song, a corny little song based on three chords — G, G7 and C. A little later we had a piano and I used to bang around on that. I wrote 'When I'm Sixty-Four' when I was about 16. I wrote the tune for that and I was vaguely thinking then it might come in handy in a musical comedy or something. I didn't know what kind of career I was going to take.

So I wrote that on piano and from there it's really been a mixture of the both. I just do either, now. Sometimes I've got a guitar in my hands; sometimes I'm sittin' at a piano. It depends whatever instrument I'm at — I'll compose on it, you know.

Every time it's different. 'All My Loving' — an old Beatle song, remember that one, folks? — I wrote that one like a bit of poetry, and then I put a song to it later. Something like 'Yesterday', I did the tune first and wrote words to that later. I called that 'Scrambled Egg' for a long time. I didn't have any words to it.

So then I got words to that; so I say, every time is different, really. I like to keep it that way, too; I don't get any set formula. So that each time, I'm pullin' it out of the air.

First of all, I was just playing it through for everyone — saying, how do you like this song? I played it just me on acoustic, and sang it. And the rest of the Beatles said, "That's it. Love it." So George Martin and I got together and sort of cooked up this idea. I wanted just a small string arrangement. And he said, "Well, how about your actual string quartet?" I said great, it sounds great. We sat down at a piano and cooked that one up.

John Lennon: As kids we were all opposed to folk-songs because they were so middle-class. It was all the college students with big scarves and a pint of beer in their hands singing folk songs in what we call la-di-da voices — "I worked in a mine in New-cast-le" and all that shit. There were very few real folk singers you know, though I liked Dominic Behan a bit and there was some good stuff to be heard in Liverpool. Just occasionally you hear very old records on the radio or TV of real workers in Ireland or somewhere singing these songs and the power of them is fantastic. But mostly folk music is people with fruity voices trying to keep alive something that's old and dead. It's all a bit boring like ballet, a minority thing kept going by a minority group. Today's folk song is Rock and Roll. Although it happened to emanate from America, that's not really important in the end because we wrote our own music and that changed everything . . . When I started, Rock and Roll itself was the basic revolution to people of my age and situation. We needed something loud and clear to break through all the unfeeling and repression that had been coming down on us kids. We were a bit conscious to begin with of being imitation Americans. But we delved into music and found that it was half white Country-and-Western and half black rhythm and blues. Most of the songs came from Europe and Africa and now they were coming back to us. Many of Dylan's best songs came from Scotland, Ireland, and England. It was a sort of cultural exchange. Though I must say the more interesting songs to me were the black ones because they were more simple. They sort of said shake your arse or your prick which was an innovation really. And then there were the field songs, mainly expressing the pain they were in. They couldn't express themselves intellectually so they had to say in a very few words what was happening to them. And then there was the City blues and a lot of that was about sex and fighting. A lot of this was self-expression but only in the last few years have they expressed themselves completely with Black Power, like Edwin Starr making War records. Before that many black singers were still labouring under that problem of God, it was often, "God will save us". But right through the blacks were singing about their pain and also about sex, which is why I like it.

John Lennon: Theory is for the critic or the audience. The experience itself is for the artist and for the audience that isn't theorising about it. That's what valid. For me criticism doesn't exist. It affects me if you say "What a terrible song you wrote" and "What a great song you wrote", it's going to affect me like if you say, "I don't like your suit". It's not that important and the

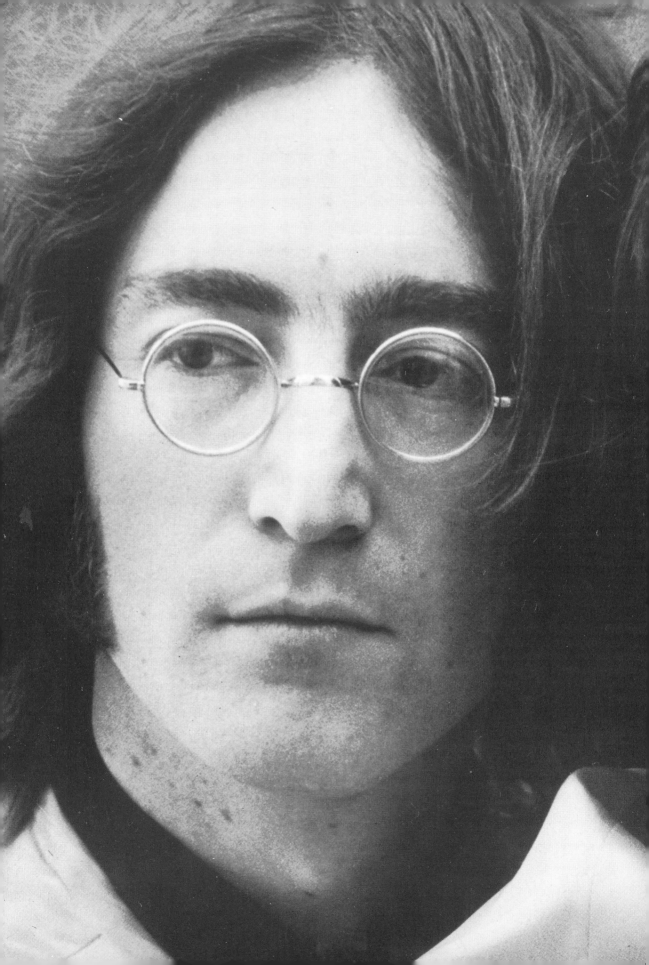

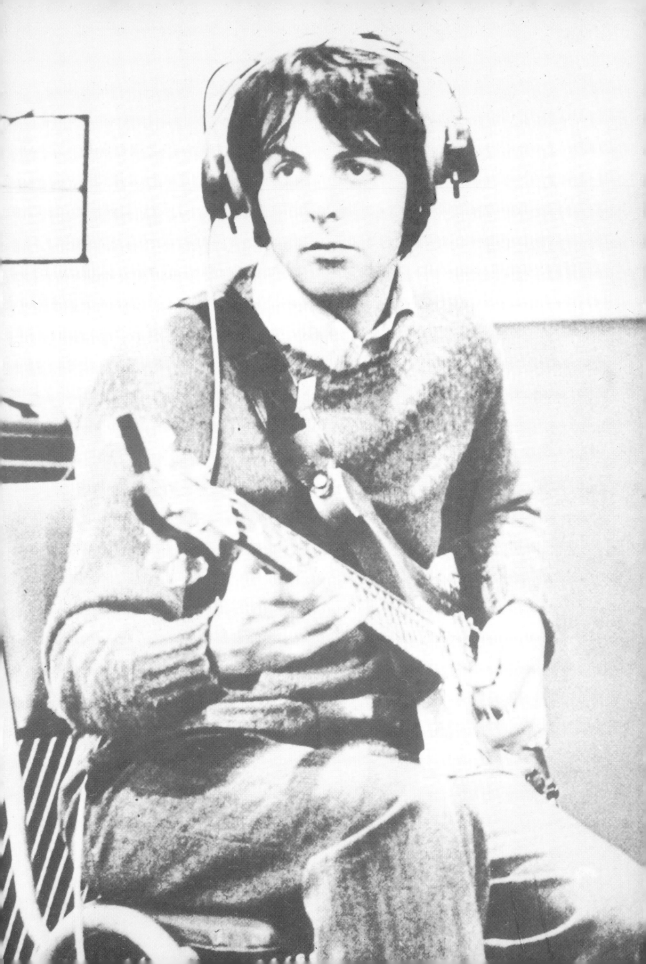

experience itself, of just hearing the music or experiencing the film is the thing. You can't relate the two. I can't be objective about it.

John Lennon: Beatlemusic is when we all get together. You know, if I want to sound like 'Come Together' and 'I Want You' all the time, which I always did and always do, or whatever it is I want to be — and Paul wants it to be whatever he wants it to be and George, etc. etc.

So when the combination works you come out with what we call Beatlemusic. Of course we don't write songs together any more. We haven't written together for two years. Not really, anyway . . . you know occasional bits, a line or two. It doesn't make any odds. When the Beatles perform that makes it into Beatlemusic.

I mean it's a long time since we've sat down and written for many reasons. We used to write mainly on tours. We got bored, so we wrote. Today the Beatles just go into a studio. And IT happens!

John Lennon: We sometimes wrote together. All our best work — apart from the early days, like 'I Want to Hold Your Hand' we wrote together and things like that — we wrote apart always. The 'One After 909', on the *Let It Be* LP, I wrote when I was 17 or 18. We always wrote separately, but we wrote together because we enjoyed it a lot sometimes, and also because they would say well, you're going to make an album get together and knock off a few songs, just like a job.

John Lennon: Well what's there to sing about? On *Abbey Road* I sing about 'Mean Mister Mustard' and 'Polythene Pam', but those are only bits of crap I wrote in India. When I get down to it I'm only interested in Yoko and Peace so if I can sing about them again and again and again, it's only, like I'm going through my blue period as a painter. That he is going to paint this cup for a year in order to go into it, get right into that cup. So maybe I'm doing that, and I'll do that until I get tried. I can always write 'Mister Kite' and those songs any time of the day. When I get down to it I like funky music. I like Rock or Blues, so what I can say in that given area I'll have to see. On *24 Hours* [a BBC TV programme] they just sardonically read the 'I Want You' lyrics: "I Want You. She's So Heavy", that's all it says, but to me that's a damn sight better than 'Walrus' or 'Eleanor Rigby' lyric-wise because it's a progression to me. If I want to write songs with no words or one word then maybe that's Yoko's influence. But when I get down to it, Bop-bop-a-Lula's great, that's what I'm getting round to.

See I remember in the early meetings with Dylan: Dylan was always saying to me, "Listen to the words, man!" and I said, "I can't be bothered. I listen to the sound of it, the sound of

the overall thing." Then I reversed that and started being a words man. I naturally play with words anyway, so I made a conscious effort to be wordy *à-la*-Dylan. But now I've relieved myself of that burden and I'm only interested in pure sound.

I don't write for the Beatles. I write for meself, so I'm influenced by whatever's going on at the time. When you write something it shows where you're at. I'm in love with Yoko, so everytime I pick up a guitar I sing about Yoko. That's how I'm

influenced. Obviously I'm influenced by her ideas and her coming from that other field: the avant-garde or underground or wherever she came from. She came in through the bathroom window!

You see I think one note is as complex as anything, but I can't go on for the rest of my life explaining that to musical critics who want complex musical harmonies, tonal cadences and all that crap. I'm a primitive so I don't need it you know. I'm not interested in that and . . . it was quite flattering at the time to hear all that crap about the Beatles, but I don't believe it. And Paul himself said that in the end we'll end up with a one note pop song. And I believe it you know! I can groove to the sound of

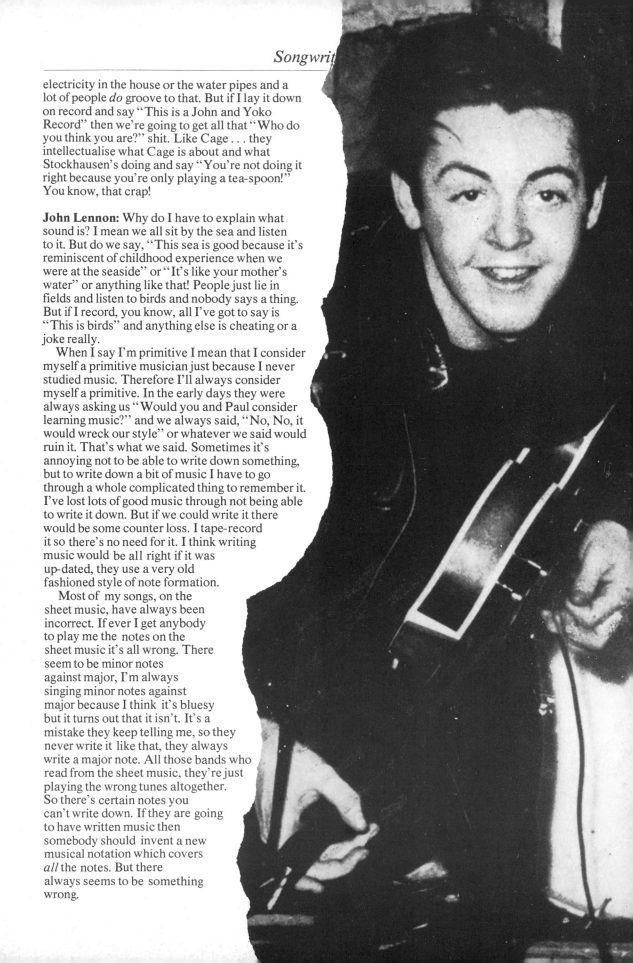

electricity in the house or the water pipes and a lot of people *do* groove to that. But if I lay it down on record and say "This is a John and Yoko Record" then we're going to get all that "Who do you think you are?" shit. Like Cage . . . they intellectualise what Cage is about and what Stockhausen's doing and say "You're not doing it right because you're only playing a tea-spoon!" You know, that crap!

John Lennon: Why do I have to explain what sound is? I mean we all sit by the sea and listen to it. But do we say, "This sea is good because it's reminiscent of childhood experience when we were at the seaside" or "It's like your mother's water" or anything like that! People just lie in fields and listen to birds and nobody says a thing. But if I record, you know, all I've got to say is "This is birds" and anything else is cheating or a joke really.

When I say I'm primitive I mean that I consider myself a primitive musician just because I never studied music. Therefore I'll always consider myself a primitive. In the early days they were always asking us "Would you and Paul consider learning music?" and we always said, "No, No, it would wreck our style" or whatever we said would ruin it. That's what we said. Sometimes it's annoying not to be able to write down something, but to write down a bit of music I have to go through a whole complicated thing to remember it. I've lost lots of good music through not being able to write it down. But if we could write it there would be some counter loss. I tape-record it so there's no need for it. I think writing music would be all right if it was up-dated, they use a very old fashioned style of note formation.

Most of my songs, on the sheet music, have always been incorrect. If ever I get anybody to play me the notes on the sheet music it's all wrong. There seem to be minor notes against major, I'm always singing minor notes against major because I think it's bluesy but it turns out that it isn't. It's a mistake they keep telling me, so they never write it like that, they always write a major note. All those bands who read from the sheet music, they're just playing the wrong tunes altogether. So there's certain notes you can't write down. If they are going to have written music then somebody should invent a new musical notation which covers *all* the notes. But there always seems to be something wrong.

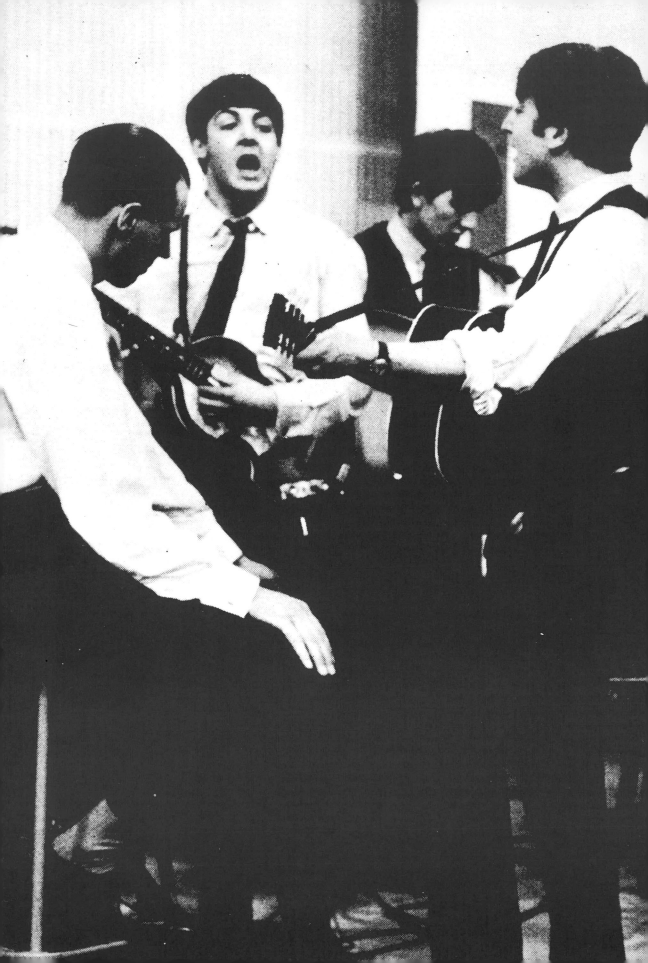

The Songs.

'Love Me Do.'

Paul McCartney: You get to the bit where you think, if we're going to write great philosophy it isn't worth it. 'Love Me Do' was our greatest philosophical song: "Love me do/you know I love you/I'll always be true/So love me do/Please love me, do." For it to be simple, and true, means that it's incredibly simple.

'Please Please Me.'

Paul McCartney: George Martin's contribution was quite a big one, actually. The first time he really ever showed that he could see beyond what we were offering him was 'Please Please Me'. It was originally conceived as a Roy Orbison-type thing, you know. George Martin said, 'Well, we'll put the tempo up.' He lifted the tempo and we all thought that was much better and that was a big hit.

'Do You Want To Know A Secret.'

John Lennon: I wrote this one. I remember getting the idea from a Walt Disney film — *Cinderella* or *Fantasia*. It went something like: "D'you wanna know a secret, promise not to tell, standing by a wishing well".

'From Me To You.'

John Lennon: Paul and I wrote this when we were on tour. We nearly didn't record it because we thought it was too bluesy at first, but when we'd finished it and George Martin had scored it with harmonica it was all right.

'Thank You Girl.'

John Lennon: Paul and I wrote this as a B-side for one of our first records. In the old days we used to write and write all the time, but nowadays I only do it if I'm particularly inspired.

'Hello Little Girl.'

Released by The Fourmost.

John Lennon: This was one of the first songs I ever finished. I was then about eighteen and we gave it to the Fourmost. I think it was the first song of my own that I ever attempted to do with the group.

'It Won't Be Long.'

John Lennon: Another early one. When I was in therapy in California they made me go through every lyric of every song I'd ever written. I couldn't believe I'd written so many songs.

'Not A Second Time.'

John Lennon: I wrote this for the second album, and it was the one that William Mann wrote about in *The Times*. He went on about the flat sub-mediant key switches and the Aeolian cadence at the end being like Mahler's *Song of the Earth*. Really it was just chords like any other chords. That was the first time anyone had written anything like that about us.

'I Call Your Name.'

John Lennon: I like this one. I wrote it very early on when I was in Liverpool, and added the middle eight when we came down to London.

'I'm Happy Just To Dance With You.'

John Lennon: I wrote this for George to sing. I'm always reading how Paul and I used to make him invisible or keep him out, but it isn't true. I encouraged him like mad.

'I'll Cry Instead.'

John Lennon: We were going to do this in *A Hard Day's Night* but the director Dick Lester didn't like it, so we put it on the flip side of the album. I like it.

'Any Time At All.'

John Lennon: Another of those songs we wrote about the time of *A Hard Day's Night*. I don't write in the same way anymore, but I suppose I could if I tried.

'You Can't Do That.'

John Lennon: This was my attempt at being Wilson Pickett at the time, but it was on the flip side because 'Can't Buy Me Love' was so good.

'I'll Be Back.'

John Lennon: An early favourite that I wrote.

'Can't Buy Me Love.'

Paul McCartney: Personally, I think you can put any interpretation you want on anything, but when someone suggests that 'Can't Buy Me Love' is about a prostitute, I draw the line. That's going too far.

'I Feel Fine.'

John Lennon: I wrote this at a recording session. It was tied together around the guitar riff that opens it.

'I Don't Want To Spoil The Party.'

John Lennon: That was a very personal one of mine. In the early days I wrote less material than Paul because he was more competent on guitar than I. He taught me quite a lot of guitar really.

'Help.'

John Lennon: I meant it — it's real. The lyric is as good now as it was then. It is no different, and it makes me feel secure to know that I was that aware of myself then. It was just me singing "Help!" and I meant it.

I don't like the recording that much; we did it too fast trying to be commercial. I like 'I Want To Hold Your Hand'. We wrote that together, it's a beautiful melody. I might do 'I Want To Hold Your Hand' and 'Help' again, because I like them and I can sing them. 'Strawberry Fields' because it's real, real for then, and I think it's like talking, 'You know, I sometimes think no . . .' It's like he talks to himself, sort of singing, which I thought was nice.

I like 'Across The Universe', too. It's one of the best lyrics I've written. In fact, it could be the best. It's good poetry, or whatever you call it, without chewin' it. See, the ones I like are the ones that stand as words, without melody. They don't have to have any melody, like a poem, you can read them.

'You've Got To Hide Your Love Away.'

John Lennon: This was written in my Dylan days for the film *Help*. When I was a teenager I used to write poetry, but was always trying to hide my real feelings.

I was in Kenwood and I would just be songwriting and so every day I would attempt to write a song and it's one of those that you sort of sing a bit sadly to yourself, "Here I stand, head in hand . . "

I started thinking about my own emotions —

I don't know when exactly it started like 'I'm a Loser' or 'Hide Your Love Away' or those kind of things — instead of projecting myself into a situation I would just try to express what I felt about myself which I'd done in me books. I think it was Dylan helped me realise that — not by any discussion or anything but just my hearing his work — I had a sort of professional songwriter's attitude to writing pop songs; he would turn out a certain style of song for a single and we would do a certain style of thing for this and the other thing. I was already a stylized songwriter on the first album. But to express myself I would write *Spaniard in the Works* or *In His Own Write*, the personal stories which were expressive of my personal emotions. I'd have a separate song-writing John Lennon who wrote songs for the sort of meat market, and I didn't consider them — the lyrics or anything — to have any depth at all. They were just a joke. Then I started being me about the songs, not writing them objectively, but subjectively.

The 'Rubber Soul' Album.

John Lennon: We were just getting better, technically and musically, that's all. Finally we took over the studio. In the early days, we had to take what we were given, we didn't know how you can get more bass. We were learning the technique on *Rubber Soul*. We were more precise about making the album, that's all, and we took over the cover and everything. That was Paul's title, it was like "Yer Blues". I suppose, meaning English Soul, I suppose, just a pun. There is no great mysterious meaning behind all of this, it was just four boys working out what to call a new album. You never know 'til you hear the song yourself. I would double track the guitar or the voice or something on the tape. I think on 'Norwegian Wood' and 'In My Life' Paul helped with the middle eight, to give credit where it's due.

From the same period, same time, I never liked 'Run For Your Life', because it was a song I just knocked off. It was inspired from — this is a very vague connection — from 'Baby Let's Play House'. There was a line on it — I used to like specific lines from songs — 'I'd rather see you dead, little girl, than to be with another man' — so I wrote it around that but I didn't think it was that important. 'Girl' I liked because I was, in a way, trying to say something or other about Christianity which I was opposed to at the time.

'Norwegian Wood.'

John Lennon: I was trying to write about an affair without letting me wife know I was writing about an affair, so it was very gobbledegook. I was sort of writing from my

experiences, girls' flats, things like that.

I wrote it at Kenwood. George had just got the sitar and I said "Could you play this piece?" We went through many different sort of versions of the song, it was never right and I was getting very angry about it, it wasn't coming out like I said. They said, "Well just do it how you want to do it." And I said, "Well I just want to do it like this." They let me go and I did the guitar very loudly into the mike and sang it at the same time and then George had the sitar and I asked him could he play the piece that I'd written, you know, dee diddley dee diddley dee, that bit, and he was not sure whether he could play it yet because he hadn't done much on the sitar but he was willing to have a go, as is his wont, and he learned the bit and dubbed it on after. I think we did it in sections.

'Nowhere Man.'

John Lennon: I was just sitting, trying to think of a song, and I thought of myself sitting there, doing nothing and getting nowhere. Once I'd thought of that, it was easy. It all came out. No, I remember now, I'd actually stopped trying to think of something. Nothing would come. I was cheesed off and went for a lie down, having given up. Then I thought of myself as "Nowhere Man" — sitting in his nowhere land.

'What Goes On.'

Ringo Starr: I used to wish that I could write songs like the others — and I've tried, but I just can't. I can get the words all right, but whenever I think of a tune and sing it to the others they always say "Yeah, it sounds like such-a-thing," and when they point it out I see what they mean. But I did get a part credit as a composer on one — it was called 'What Goes On'.

'In My Life.'

John Lennon: I wrote that in Kenwood. I used to write upstairs where I had about ten Brunell tape recorders all linked up, I still have them, I'd mastered them over the period of a year or two — I could never make a rock and roll record but I could make some far out stuff on it. I wrote it upstairs, that was one where I wrote the lyrics first and then sang it. That was usually the case with things like 'In My Life' and 'Universe' and some of the ones that stand out a bit.

'Girl.'

John Lennon: This was about dream girl. When Paul and I wrote lyrics in the old days we used to laugh about it like the Tin Pan Alley people would. And it was only later on that we tried to match the lyrics to the tune. I like this one. It was one of my best.

'Run For Your Life.'

John Lennon: I always hated 'Run For Your Life.'

'Eleanor Rigby.'

Paul McCartney: Well that started off with sitting down at the piano and getting the first line of the melody, and playing around with words. I think it was 'Miss Daisy Hawkins' originally; then it was her picking up the rice in a church after a wedding. That's how nearly all our songs start, with the first line just suggesting itself from books or newspapers.

At first I thought it was a young Miss Daisy Hawkins, a bit like 'Annabel Lee', but not so sexy; but then I saw I'd said she was picking up the rice in church, so she had to be a cleaner; she had missed the wedding, and she was suddenly lonely. In fact she had missed it all — she was the spinster type.

Jane [Asher] was in a play in Bristol then, and I was walking round the streets waiting for her to finish. I didn't really like 'Daisy Hawkins' — I wanted a name that was more real. The thought just came: "Eleanor Rigby picks up the rice and lives in a dream" — so there she was. The next thing was Father Mackenzie. It was going to be Father McCartney, but then I thought that was a bit of a hang-up for my Dad, being in this lonely song. So we looked through the phone book. That's the beauty of working at random — it does come up perfectly, much better than if you try to think it with your intellect.

Anyway there was Father Mackenzie, and he was just as I had imagined him, lonely, darning his socks. We weren't sure if the song was going to go on. In the next verse we thought of a bin man, an old feller going through dustbins; but it got too involved — embarrassing. John and I wondered whether to have Eleanor Rigby and him have a thing going, but we couldn't really see how. When I played it to John we decided to finish it.

That was the point anyway. She didn't make it, she never made it with anyone, she didn't even look as if she was going to.

'Yellow Submarine.'

Paul McCartney: I knew it would get connotations, but it really was a children's song. I just loved the idea of kids singing it. With 'Yellow Submarine' the whole idea was "If someday I came across some kids singing it, that will be it", so it's got to be very easy — there isn't a single big word. Kids will understand it easier than adults. "In the town where I was born/there lived a man who sailed to sea/And he told of his life in the land of submarines."

That's really the beginning of a kids' story. There's some stuff in Greece like icing sugar — you eat it. It's like a sweet and you drop it into water. It's called submarine; we had it on holiday.

What about the lyrics to 'Yellow Submarine'? Is there an allusion to narcotics?

Ringo: Nothing at all. It's simply a children's song with no hidden meanings. Many people have interpreted it to be a war song, that eventually all the world would be living in yellow submarines. That's not the case.

'She Said, She Said'.

John Lennon: I like this one. I wrote it about an acid trip I was on in Los Angeles. It was only the second trip we'd had. We took it because we'd started hearing things about it and we wanted to know what it was all about. Peter Fonda came over to us and started saying things like "I know what it's like to be dead, man" and we didn't really wanna know, but he kept going on and on . . . Anyway that's where that song came from, and it's a nice song, too.

WITH BLUE MEANIE

'Dr. Roberts.'

Paul McCartney: Well, he's like a joke. There's some fellow in New York, and in the States we'd hear people say: "You can get everything off him; any pills you want." It was a big racket, but a joke too about this fellow who cured everyone of everything with all these pills and tranquillisers, injections for this and that; he just kept New York high. That's what 'Dr. Roberts' is all about, just a pill doctor who sees you all right. It was a joke between ourselves, but they go in in-jokes and come out out-jokes because everyone listens and puts their own thing on it, which is great. I mean, when I was young I never knew what "gilly gilly elsa feffer cats . . ." was all about, but I still enjoyed singing it. You put your own meaning at your own level to our songs and that's what's great about them.

'Got To Get You Into My Life.'

John Lennon: We were influenced by our Tamla Motown bit on this. You see we're influenced by whatever's going.

'Tomorrow Never Knows.'

John Lennon: Often the backing I think of early on never comes off. With 'Tomorrow Never Knows' I'd imagined in my head that in the background you would hear thousands of monks chanting. That was impractical of course and we did something different. I should have tried to get near my original idea, the monks singing, I realise now that was what it wanted.

'Penny Lane.'

Paul McCartney: 'Penny Lane' is a bus roundabout in Liverpool; and there is a barber's shop showing photographs of every head he's had the pleasure to know — no that's not true, they're just photos of hairstyles, but all the people who come and go/stop and say hullo. There's a bank on the corner so we made up the bit about the banker in his motor car. It's part fact, part nostalgia for a place which is a great place, blue suburban skies as we remember it, and it's still there.

And we put in a joke or two: "Four of fish and finger pie." The women would never dare say that, except to themselves. Most people wouldn't hear it, but "finger pie" is just a nice little joke for the Liverpool lads who like a bit of smut.

'Strawberry Fields.'

Paul McCartney: There's a lot of random in our songs — 'Strawberry Fields' is the name of a Salvation Army School — by the time we've taken it through the writing stage, thinking of it, playing it to the others, writing it, and letting them think of bits, recording it once and deciding it's not quite right and do it again and then find "Oh, that's it, the solo comes here and that goes there", then bang, you have the jigsaw puzzle.

That happens with all our songs, except the ones we want to keep really simple, like 'When I'm 64' and 'Fixing a Hole'.

That wasn't "I buried Paul" at all, that was John saying "cranberry sauce". It was the end of 'Strawberry Fields'. That's John's humour. John would say something totally out of synch, like 'cranberry sauce'. If you don't realise that John's apt to say 'cranberry sauce' when he feels like it, then you start to hear a funny little word there, and you think "Aha!"

Ringo Starr: Everybody thinks Paul wrote it, but John wrote it for me. He's got a lot of soul has John, you know.

The 'Sgt. Pepper' Album.

John Lennon: Sgt. Pepper is the one. It was a peak. Paul and I were definitely working together, especially on 'A Day In the Life' that was a real . . . The way we wrote a lot of the time: you'd write the good bit, the part that was easy, like "I read the news today" or whatever it was, then when you got stuck or whenever it got hard, instead of carrying on, you just drop it; then we would meet each other, and I would sing half, and he would be inspired to write the next bit and *vice versa*. He was a bit shy about it because I think he thought it's already a good song. Sometimes we wouldn't let each other interfere with a song either, because you tend to be a bit lax with someone else's stuff, you experiment a bit. So we were doing it in his room with the piano. He said "Should we do this?", "Yeah, let's do that."

I keep saying that I always preferred the double album, because *my* music is better on the double album; I don't care about the whole concept of *Pepper*, it might be better, but the music was better for me on the double album, because I'm being myself on it. I think it's as simple as the new album, like 'I'm So Tired' is just the guitar. I felt more at ease with that than the production. I don't like production so much. But *Pepper* was a peak all right.

'Sgt. Pepper's Lonely Hearts Club Band.'

Paul McCartney: I was just thinking of nice words like Sergeant Pepper, and Lonely Hearts Club, and they came together for no reason. But after you have written that down you start to think, "There's this Sergeant Pepper who has taught the band to play, and got them going so that at least they found one number. They're a bit of a brass band in a way, but also a rock band in a way, but also a rock band because they've got the San Francisco thing". And I had the idea that instead of Hell's Angels, they put up pictures of Hitler and the latest Nazi signs and leather and that. We went into it just like that: just us doing a good show.

There's no need to make things up. We started on interviewers who would say, "What do you believe?" and we'd say, "We do not believe in gold lamé suits: that's trying to glory it up and doesn't even do it well." That detaches you from the real thing. That's why Daisy Hawkins wasn't any good — it sounds like Daisy made-up. Billy Shears is another that sounds like a schoolmate but isn't. Possibly one day we'll meet all these people.

Ringo's Billy Shears. Definitely. That was just in the production of *Sgt. Pepper*. It just happened to turn out that we dreamed up Billy Shears. It was a rhyme for "years" . . . "band you've known for all these years . . . and here he is, the one and only Billy Shears." We thought, that's a great little name, it's an Eleanor-Rigby-type name, a nice atmospheric name, and it was leading into Ringo's track. So as far as we were concerned it was purely and simply a device to get the next song in.

'Lucy In The Sky With Diamonds.'

Paul McCartney: This one is amazing. As I was saying before, when you write a song and you mean it one way, and then someone comes up and says something about it that you didn't think of — you can't deny it. Like 'Lucy in the Sky with Diamonds', people came up and said, very cunningly, "Right, I get it. L—S—D" and it *was* when all the papers were talking about LSD, but we never thought about it.

What happened was that John's son Julian did a drawing at school and brought it home, and he has a schoolmate called Lucy, and John said what's that, and he said "Lucy in the Sky with Diamonds" — so we had a nice title. We did the whole thing like an Alice in Wonderland idea, being in a boat on the river, slowly drifting downstream and those great cellophane flowers towering over your head. Every so often it broke off and you saw "Lucy in the Sky with Diamonds" all over the sky. This Lucy was God, the big figure, the white rabbit. You can just write a song with imagination on *words* and that's what we did.

It's like modern poetry, but neither John nor I have read much. The last time I approached it I was thinking "This is strange and far out", and I did not dig it all that much, except Dylan

Thomas who I suddenly started getting, and I was quite pleased with myself because I got it, but I hadn't realised he was going to be saying exactly the same things.

'Fixing A Hole.'

Paul McCartney: This song is just about the hole in the road where the rain gets in; a good old analogy — the hole in your make-up which lets the rain in and stops your mind from going where it will. It's you interfering with things; as when someone walks up to you and says, "I am the Son of God". And you say, "No you're not; I'll crucify you", and you crucify him. Well that's life, but it is *not* fixing a hole.

It's about fans too: "See the people standing there/who disagree and never win/and wonder why they don't get in/Silly people, run around/they worry me/and never ask why they don't get in my door." If they only knew that the best way to get in is not to do that, because obviously anyone who is going to be straight and like a real friend and a real person to us is going to get in; but they simply stand there and give off, "We are fans, don't let us in."

Sometimes I invite them in, but it starts to be not really the point in a way, because I invited one in, and the next day she was in the *Daily Mirror* with her mother saying we were going to get married. So we tell the fans, "Forget it."

If you're a junky sitting in a room *fixing* a hole then that's what it will mean to you, but when I wrote it I meant if there's a crack or the room is uncolourful, then I'll paint it.

'She's Leaving Home.'

Paul McCartney: It's a much younger girl, than 'Eleanor Rigby', but the same sort of loneliness. That was a *Daily Mirror* story again: this girl left home and her father said: "We gave her everything, I don't know why she left home." But he didn't give her that much, not what she wanted when she left home.

'Being For The Benefit Of Mr. Kite!'

Paul McCartney: John has this old poster which says right at the top "Pablo Fanques Fair Presents the Hendersons for the benefit of Mr Kite", and it has all the bits of thing that sound strange: "Over men and horses, hoops and garters, lastly through a hogshead of real fire". "The Hendersons" — you couldn't make that up.

'Within You Without You.'

George Harrison: Klaus [Voorman] had a harmonium in his house, which I hadn't played before. I was doodling on it, playing to

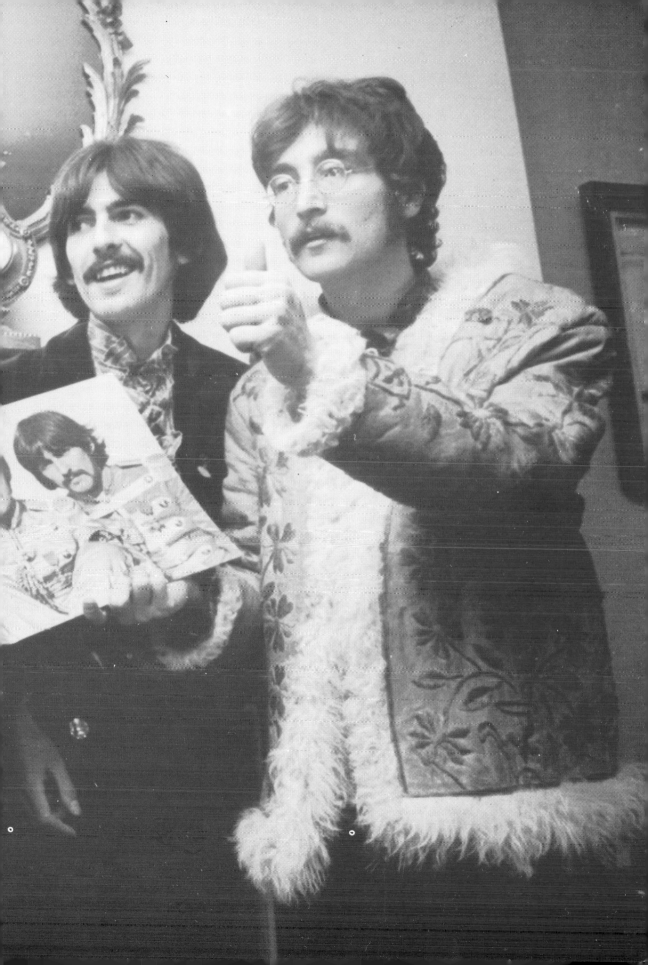

amuse myself, when 'Within You' started to come. The tune came first then I got the first sentence. It came out of what we'd been doing that evening.

'Lovely Rita'.

Paul McCartney: I was bopping about on the piano in Liverpool when someone told me that in America they call parking-meter women meter maids. I thought that was great, and it got to "Rita Meter Maid" and then "Lovely Rita Meter Maid" and I was thinking vaguely that it should be a hate song: "You took my car away and I'm so blue today". And you wouldn't be liking her; but then I thought it would be better to love her and if she was very freaky too, like a military man, with a bag on her shoulder. A foot stomper, but nice.

The song was imagining if somebody was there taking down my number and I suddenly fell for her, and the kind of person I'd be, to fall for a meter maid, would be a shy office clerk and I'd say, "May I inquire discreetly when you are free to take some tea with me". Tea, not pot. It's like saying, "Come and cut the grass" and then realising that could be pot, or the old teapot could be something about pot. But I don't mind pot and I leave the words in. They're not consciously introduced just to say pot and be clever.

'Good Morning, Good Morning'.

John Lennon: I often sit at the piano, working at songs, with the telly on low in the background. If I'm a bit low and not getting much done then the words on the telly come through. That's when I heard "Good Morning, Good Morning" . . . it was a Corn Flakes advertisement.

'A Day In The Life'.

John Lennon: I was writing the song with the *Daily Mail* propped up in front of me on the piano, I had it open at their News In Brief, or Far or Near, whatever they call it. There was a paragraph about 4,000 holes in Blackburn, Lancashire, being discovered and there was still one word missing in that verse when we came to record. I knew the line had to go "Now they know how many holes it takes to fill the Albert Hall." It was a nonsense verse really, but for some reason I couldn't think of the verb. What did the holes do to the Albert Hall? It was Terry [Doran] who said 'fill' the Albert Hall.
Paul McCartney: There'd been a story about a man who'd made the grade, and there'd been a photograph of him sitting in his car. John said, "I had to laugh". He'd sort of blown his mind out

in the car. He was just high on whatever he uses, say he was pissed in this big Bentley, sitting at the traffic lights. He's driving today, the chauffeur isn't there, and maybe he got high because of that. The lights have changed and he hasn't noticed that there's a crowd of housewives and they're all looking at him saying "Who's that. I've seen him in the papers" and they're not sure if he's from the House of Lords. He looks a bit like that with his homburg and white scarf and he's out of his screws.

That's a bit of black comedy. The next bit was another song altogether but it just happened to fit. It was just me remembering what it was like to run up the road to catch a bus to school, having a smoke and going into class. We decided: "Bugger this, we're going to write a turn-on song." It was a reflection of my school days — I would have a Woodbine then, and somebody would speak and I would go into a dream.

This was the only one in the album written as a deliberate provocation. A stick-that-in-your-pipe . . . But what we want is to turn you on to the truth rather than pot.

The 'Sgt. Pepper' Cover.

Paul McCartney: These were all just cult heroes. George chose a few of his schoolmates he liked; and the rest of us said names we liked the sound of: like Aldous Huxley, H. G. Wells, Johnny Weissmuller.

Those Indian people have amazing stories. There's one called Yogananda Para Manza, who died in 1953 and left his body in an incredibly perfect state. Medical reports in Los Angeles three or four months after he died were saying this is incredible; this man hasn't decomposed yet. He was sitting there glowing because he did this sort of transcendental bit, transcended his body by planes of consciousness. He was taught by another person on the cover and *he* was taught by *another*, and it all goes back to the one called Babujee who's just a little drawing looking upwards.

You can't photograph him — he's an agent. He puts a curse on the film. He's the all-time governor, he's been at it a long time and he's still around doing the transcending bit.

So they're there planning the spiritual thing for us. So, if they *are* planning it, what a groove that he's got himself on our cover, right in the middle of the Beatles' LP cover! Normal ideas of God wouldn't have him interested in Beatles music or *any* pop — it's a bit infra dig — but obviously, if we're all here doing it, and someone's interested in us, then it's all to do with it. There's not one bit worse than another bit. So that's great, that's beautiful, that he's right on the cover with all his mates.

Whatever it is, it's what is doing all those trees and doing us and keeping you going, which someone must be doing.

The Yogi goes through millions of things to realise the simplest of all truths, because while you are going through this part, there's always the opposite truth. You say, "Ah well, that's all there is to it then. It's all great, and God's looking after you". Then someone says, "What about a hunchback then, is that great?" And you say, "OK then, it's all lousy". And this is just as true if you want to see it. But the truth is that it's neither good nor lousy; just down the middle; a state of being that doesn't have black or white, good or bad.

We realised for the first time that someday someone would actually be holding a thing that they'd call "The Beatles' new LP" and that normally it would just be a collection of songs or a nice picture on the cover, nothing more. So the idea was to do a complete thing that you could make what you liked of; just a little magic presentation. We were going to have a little envelope in the centre with the nutty things you can buy at Woolworth's: a surprise packet.

The 'Sgt. Pepper' Critics.

Paul McCartney: Then the this-little-bit-if-you-play-it-backwards stuff. As I say, nine times out of ten it's really nothing. Take the end of *Sgt. Pepper*, that backward thing, "We'll fuck you like Supermen." Some fans came around to my door giggling. I said, "Hello, what do you want?" They said, "Is it true, that bit at the end? Is it true? It says 'We'll fuck you like Supermen'." I said, "No, you're kidding. I haven't heard it, but I'll play it." It was just some piece of conversation that was recorded and turned backwards. But I went inside after I'd seen them and played it studiously, turned it backwards with my thumb against the motor, turned the motor off and did it backwards. And there it was, sure as anything, plain as anything. "We'll fuck you like Supermen." I thought, Jesus, what can you do?

The time we got offended, I'll tell you, was one of the reviews, I think about *Sgt. Pepper* — one of the reviews said, "This is George Martin's finest album." We got shook; I mean, we don't mind him helping us, it's great, it's a great help, but it's not his album, folks, you know. And there got to be a little bitterness over that. A bit of help, but Christ, if he's goin' to get all the credit . . . for the whole album . . .

We write songs; we know what we mean by them. But in a week someone else says something about it, says that it means that as well, and you can't deny it. Things take on millions of meanings. I don't understand it.

A fantastic example is the inner track on the back of *Sergeant Pepper* that plays for hours if your automatic doesn't cut off. It's like a mantra in Yoga and the meaning changes and it all becomes dissociated from what it is saying.

You get a pure buzz after a while because it's *so* boring it ceases to mean *anything*.

'All You Need Is Love.'

Paul McCartney: George Martin always has something to do with it, but sometimes more than others. For instance, he wrote the end of 'All you need is Love' and got into trouble because the "In the Mood" bit was copyrighted. We thought of all the great clichés because they're a great bit of random. It was a hurried session and we didn't mind giving him that to do — saying "There's the end, we want it to go on and on". Actually what he wrote was much more disjointed, so when we put all the bits together we said, "Could we have 'Greensleeves' right on top of that little Bach thing?" And on top of that we had the "In the Mood" bit.

George is quite a sage. Sometimes he works with us, sometimes against us; he's always looked after us. I don't think he does as much as some people think. He sometimes does all the arrangements and we just change them.

'Lady Madonna.'

Ringo Starr: It sounds like Elvis doesn't it? No — no it doesn't sound like Elvis. It is Elvis — even those bits where he goes very high.

'Blue Jay Way.'

George Harrison: Derek [Taylor] got held up. He rang to say he'd be late. I told him on the

phone that the house was in Blue Jay Way. He said he could find it okay, he could always ask a cop.

'The Inner Light.'

Paul McCartney: George wrote this. Forget the Indian music and listen to the melody. Don't you think it's a beautiful melody? It's really lovely.

'Hey Jude.'

Paul McCartney: I happened to be driving out to see Cynthia Lennon. I think it was just after John and she had broken up, and I was quite mates with Julian [their son]. He's a nice kid, Julian. And I was going out in me car just vaguely singing this song, and it was like "Hey Jules". I don't know why, "Hey Jules". It was just this thing, you know, "Don't make it bad/Take a sad song . . ." And then I just thought a better name was Jude. A bit more country and western for me.

Once you get analyzing something and looking into it, things *do* begin to appear and things *do* begin to tie in. Because *everything* ties in, and what you get depends on your approach to it. You look at everything with a black attitude and it's all black.

'Revolution.'

John Lennon: When George and Paul and all of them were on holiday, I made 'Revolution' which is on the LP and 'Revolution #9'. I wanted to put it out as a single, I had it all prepared, but they came by, and said it wasn't good enough. And we put out what? 'Hello Goodbye' or some shit like that? No, we put out 'Hey Jude', which was worth it — I'm sorry — but we could have had both.

I wanted to put what I felt about revolution; I thought it was time we fuckin' spoke about it, the same as I thought it was about time we stopped not answering about the Vietnamese War when we were on tour with Brian Epstein and had to tell him, "We're going to talk about the war this time and we're not going to just waffle". I wanted to say what I thought about revolution.

I had been thinking about it up in the hills in India. I still had this "God will save us" feeling about it, that it's going to be all right (even now I'm saying "Hold on, John, it's going to be all right", otherwise, I won't hold on) but that's why I did it, I wanted to talk, I wanted to say my piece about revolution. I wanted to tell you, or whoever listens, to communicate, to say, "What do you say? This is what I say."

On one version I said "Count me in" about violence, in or out, because I wasn't sure. But the version we put out said "Count me out", because I don't fancy a violent revolution happening all over. I don't want to die; but I begin to think what else can happen, you know, it seems inevitable.

'Revolution #9' was an unconscious picture of what I actually think will happen when it happens: that was just like a drawing of revolution. All the thing was made with loops. I had about thirty loops going, fed them onto one basic track. I was getting classical tapes, going upstairs and chopping them up, making it backwards and things like that, to get the sound effects. One thing was an engineer's testing tape and it would come on with a voice saying "This is EMI Test Series #9." I just cut up whatever he said and I'd number nine it. Nine turned out to be my birthday and my lucky number and everything. I didn't realize it; it was just so funny the voice saying "Number nine"; it was like a joke, bringing number nine into it all the time, that's all it was.

Yoko: It also turns out to be the highest number you know, one, two, etc., up to nine.

John: There are many symbolic things about it but it just happened you know, just an engineer's tape and I was just using all the bits to make a montage. I really wanted that released.

So that's my feeling. The idea was don't aggravate the pig by waving the thing that aggravates — by waving the Red flag in his face. You know, I really thought that love would save us all. But now I'm wearing a Chairman Mao badge. I'm just beginning to think he's doing a good job. I would never know until I went to China. I'm not going to be like that. I was just always interested enough to sing about him. I just wondered what the kids who were actually Maoists were doing. I wondered what their motive was and what was really going on. I thought if they wanted revolution, if they really want to be subtle, what's the point of saying "I'm a Maoist and why don't you shoot me down?" I thought that wasn't a very clever way of getting what they wanted.

John Lennon: Ah, sure, 'Revolution'. There were two versions of that song but the underground left only picked up on the one that said "Count me out". The original version which ends up on the LP said "count me in" too; I put in both because I wasn't sure. There was a third version that was just abstract, musique concrete, kinds of loops and that, people screaming. I thought I was painting in sound a picture of revolution — but I made a mistake, you know. The mistake was that it was anti-revolution. On the version released as a single I said "When you talk about destruction you can count me out". I didn't want to get killed. I didn't really know that much about the Maoists, but I just knew that they seemed to be so few and yet they painted themselves green and stood in front of the police waiting to get picked off. I just thought it was unsubtle, you know.

I thought the original Communist revolutionaries coordinated themselves a bit better and didn't go around shouting about it. That was how I felt — I was really asking a question. As someone from the working class I was always interested in Russia and China and everything that related to the working class, even though I was playing the capitalist game. At one time I was so much involved in the religious bullshit that I used to go around describing myself as a Christian Communist, but as Janov says, religion is legalized madness. It was therapy that stripped away all that made me feel my pain won.

'Glass Onion'.

John Lennon: I was having a laugh because there'd been so much gobbledegook about *Pepper*, play it backwards and you stand on your head and all that. Even now, I just saw Mel Torme on TV the other day saying that 'Lucy' was written to promote drugs and so was 'A Little Help From My Friends' and none of them were at all — 'A Little Help From My Friends' only says get high in it, it's really about a little help from my friends, it's a sincere message. Paul had the line about "little help from my friends", I'm not sure, he had some kind of structure for it and — we wrote it pretty well 50-50 but it was based on his original idea.

'Wild Honey Pie'.

Paul McCartney: This was just a fragment of an instrumental which we weren't sure about, but Patti liked it very much so we decided to leave it on the album.

'Happiness Is A Warm Gun'.

John Lennon: Oh, I like that, one of my best, I had forgotten about that. Oh, I love it. I think it's a beautiful song. I like all the different things that are happening in it. Like "God", I had put together some three sections of different songs, it was meant to be — it seemed to run through all the different kinds of rock music.

It wasn't about "H" at all. 'Lucy In The Sky With Diamonds' which I swear to God, or swear to Mao, or to anybody you like, I had no idea spelled L.S.D. — and 'Happiness' — George Martin had a book on guns which he had told me about — I can't remember — or I think he showed me a cover of a magazine that said "Happiness Is A Warm Gun". It was a gun magazine, that's it: I read it, thought it was a fantastic, insane thing to say. A warm gun means that you just shot something.

Paul McCartney: I think this is my favourite on The Beatles album.

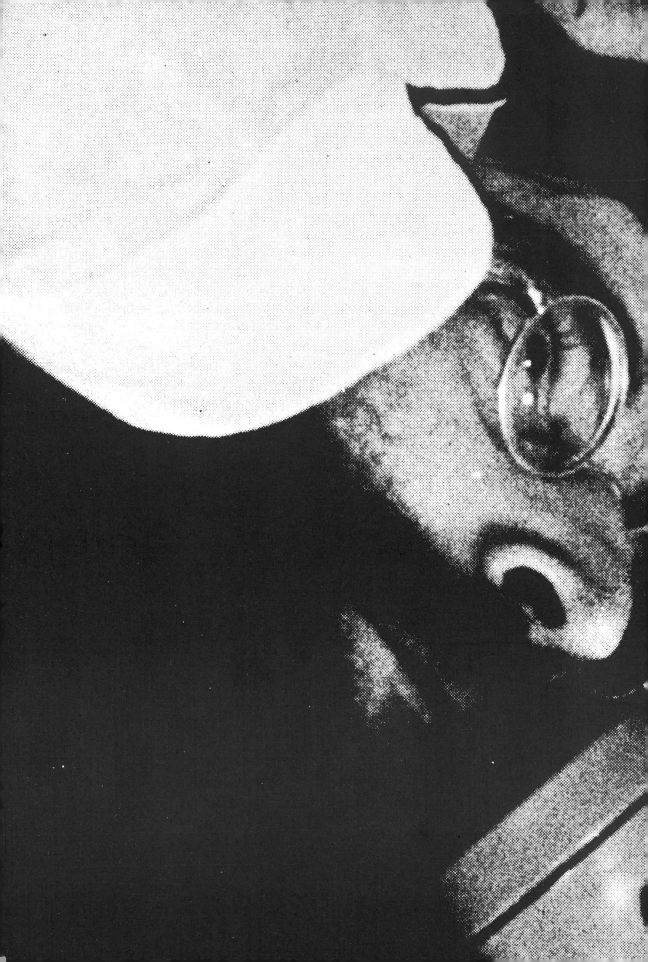

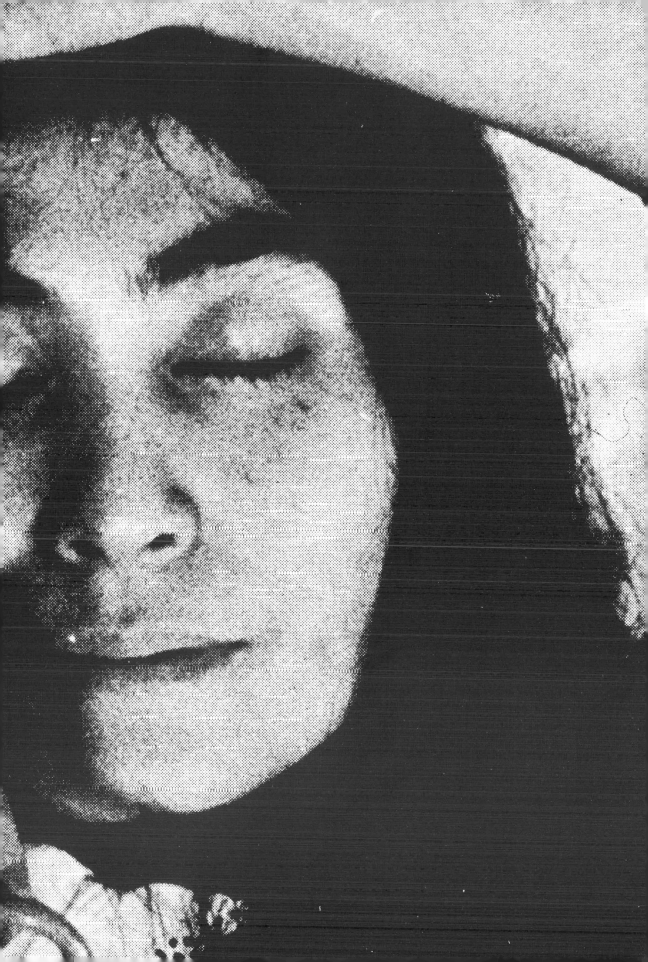

'Hey Bulldog.'

John Lennon: Paul said we should do a real song in the studio, to save wasting time. Could I whip one off? I had a few words at home so I brought them in.

'The Ballad Of John And Yoko.'

John Lennon: How can I be lonely when I'm with Yoko day and night? I'm lonely in the universal sense, but there are no outside desires. We are the best things we can give each other.

'Give Peace A Chance.'

Released by Plastic Ono Band.
John Lennon: The real word I used on the record was "masturbation", but I'd just got in trouble for 'The Ballad of John and Yoko' and I didn't want any more fuss, so I put "mastication" in the written lyrics. It was a cop-out, but the message about peace was more important to me than having a little laugh about a word.

The 'Abbey Road' Album.

John Lennon: I liked the "A" side but I never liked that sort of pop opera on the other side. I think it's junk because it was just bits of songs thrown together. 'Come Together' is all right, that's all I remember. That was my song. It was a competent album, like *Rubber Soul*. It was together in that way, but *Abbey Road* had no life in it.

On Abbey Road *you go back to some pretty early Rock stuff.*
John Lennon: Well we always do. I mean 'Lady Madonna' etcetera. We never went away from it. There isn't a Beatle album without some Rock and Roll on it is there? There isn't one that I can think of. I mean, 'Sgt. Pepper' is a Rock and Roll song, and 'Good Morning Good Morning' was fairly straight Rock and Roll except for some strange beats on it. Sounds Incorporated playing their saxes and all that.

'Come Together.'

John Lennon: This is another of my favourites. It was intended as a campaign song at first, but it never turned out that way. People often ask how I write: I do it in all kinds of ways — with piano, guitar, any combination you can think of, in fact. It isn't easy.

'Maxwell's Silver Hammer.'

Paul McCartney: This epitomises the downfalls in life. Just when everything is going smoothly "bang bang" down comes Maxwell's silver hammer and ruins everything.

'Oh! Darling.'

Paul McCartney: When we were recording this track I came into the studios early every day for a week to sing it by myself because at first my voice was too clear. I wanted it to sound as though I'd been performing it on stage all week.

'I Want You.'

John Lennon: This is about Yoko. She's very heavy, and there was nothing else I could say about her other than I want you, she's so heavy. Someone said the lyrics weren't very good. But there was nothing more I wanted to say.

I remember that the simplicity on the new album was evident on the Beatles double album. It was evident in 'She's So Heavy', in fact a reviewer wrote of 'She's So Heavy': "He seems to have lost his talent for lyrics, it's so simple and boring". 'She's So Heavy' was about Yoko. When it gets down to it, like she said, when you're drowning you don't say "I would be incredibly pleased if someone would have the foresight to notice me drowning and come and help me", you just *scream*. And in 'She's So Heavy', I just sang "I want you, I want you so bad, she's so heavy, I want you", like that. I started simplifying my lyrics then, on the double album.

'Because.'

John Lennon: This is about me and Yoko in the early days. Yoko was playing some Beethoven chords and I said play them backwards. It's really *Moonlight Sonata* backwards.

'Mean Mr. Mustard.'

John Lennon: This was just one of those written in India.

'Polythene Pam.'

John Lennon: I wrote this one in India, and when I recorded it I used a thick Liverpool accent because it was supposed to be about a mythical Liverpool scrubber dressed up in her jackboots and kilt.

'She Came In Through The Bathroom Window.'

Paul McCartney: This forms part of a medley of songs which is about 15 minutes long on *Abbey Road*. We did it this way because both John and I had a number of songs which were great as they were but which we'd never finished.

'Golden Slumbers'.

Paul McCartney: I was at my father's house in Cheshire messing about on the piano and I came across the traditional tune 'Golden Slumbers' in a song book of Ruth's [his stepsister]. And I thought it would be nice to write my own 'Golden Slumbers'.

'Cold Turkey'.

Released by Plastic Ono Band.
John Lennon: I wrote this about coming off drugs and the pain involved.

The 'Let It Be' Album.

John Lennon: It was another one like *Magical Mystery Tour*. In a nutshell, it was time for another Beatle movie or something; Paul wanted us to go on the road or do something. He sort of set it up, and there were discussions about where to go, and all that. I had Yoko by then, and I would just tag along. I was stoned all the time and I just didn't give a shit. Nobody did. It was just like it was in the movie; when I got to do 'Across The Universe' (which I wanted to record because the original wasn't very good), Paul yawns and plays boogie. I merely say, "Anyone want to do a fast one?" That's how I am. Year after year, that begins to wear you down.

Paul had this idea that he was going to rehearse us. He's looking for perfection all the time, and had these ideas that we would rehearse and then make the album. We, being lazy fuckers — and we'd been playing for 20 years! We're grown men, for fuck's sake, and we're not going to sit around and rehearse, I'm not, anyway — we couldn't get into it.

We put down a few tracks, and nobody was in it at all. It just was a dreadful, dreadful feeling in Twickenham Studio, being filmed all the time, I just wanted them to go away. We'd be there at eight in the morning. You couldn't make music at eight in the morning in a strange place, with people filming you, and coloured lights flashing.

The tape ended up like the bootleg version. We didn't want to know about it anymore, so we just left it to Glyn Johns and said, "Here, mix it". That was the first time since the first album that we didn't want to have anything to do with it. None of us could be bothered going in. Nobody called anybody about it, and the tapes were left there. Glyn Johns did it. We got an acetate in the mail and we called each other and said, "What do you think?".

We were going to let it out in really shitty condition. I didn't care. I thought it was good to let it out and show people what had happened to us, we can't get it together; we don't play together any more; you know, leave us alone.

PHIL SPECTOR

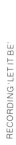

The bootleg version is what it was like, and everyone was probably thinking they're not going to fucking work on it. There were 29 hours of tape, so much that it was like a movie. Twenty takes of everything, because we were rehearsing and taking everything. Nobody could face looking at it.

When Spector came around, we said, "Well, if you want to work with us, go and do your audition". He worked like a pig on it. He always wanted to work with the Beatles, and he was given the shittiest load of badly recorded shit, with a lousy feeling toward it, ever. And he made something out of it. He did a great job.

When I heard it, I didn't puke; I was so relieved after six months of this black cloud hanging over me that this was going to go out.

I had thought it would be good to let the shitty version out because it would break the Beatles, break the myth. It would be just us, with no trousers on and no glossy paint over the cover, and no hype: "This is what we are like with our trousers off would you please end the game now?".

But that didn't happen. We ended up doing *Abbey Road* quickly, and putting out something slick to preserve the myth. I am weak as well as strong, you know, and I wasn't going to fight for *Let It Be* because I really couldn't stand it.

'Get Back'.

Paul McCartney: We were sitting in the studio and we made it up out of thin air . . . we started to write words there and then . . . when we finished it, we recorded it at Apple Studios and made it into a song to roller-coast by.

'Across The Universe'.

John Lennon: This was one of my favourite songs, but it's been issued in so many forms that it's missed it as a record. I gave it at first to the World Wild Life Fund, but they didn't do much with it, and then we put it on the *Let It Be* album.

'One After 909'.

John Lennon: One of the first songs I ever wrote, which we revived for the film *Let It Be*.

The Films.

Do you like making movies?
Paul: It's not a bad way to get through an afternoon.

A Hard Day's Night.

John Lennon: I dug *Hard Day's Night*, although Alun Owen only came with us for two days before he wrote the script. He invented that word "grotty" — did you know that?

We thought the word was really weird, and George curled up with embarrassment every time he had to say it.

But it's part of the language now — you hear society people using it. Amazing.

John Lennon: The story wasn't bad but it could have been better. Another illusion was that we were just puppets and that these great people, like Brian Epstein and Dick Lester, created the situation and made this whole fuckin' thing, and *precisely* because we were what we were, realistic. We didn't want to make a fuckin' shitty pop movie, we didn't want to make a movie that was going to be bad, and we insisted on having a real writer to write it.

Brian came up with Alun Owen, from Liverpool, who had written a play for TV called *No Trams to Lime St.* Lime Street is a famous street in Liverpool where the whores used to be in the old days, and Owen was famous for writing Liverpool dialogue. We auditioned people to write for us and they came up with this guy. He was a bit phony, like a professional Liverpool man — you know like a professional American. He stayed with us two days, and wrote the whole thing based on our characters then: me, witty; Ringo, dumb and cute; George this; and Paul that.

We were a bit infuriated by the glibness and shiftiness of the dialogue and we were always trying to get it more realistic, but they wouldn't have it. It ended up O.K., but the next one was just bullshit, because it really had *nothing* to do with the Beatles. They just put us here and there. Dick Lester was good, he had ideas ahead of their times, like using Batman comic strip lettering and balloons.

It was a good projection of one façade of us, which was on tour, once in London and once in Dublin. It was of us in that situation together, in a hotel, having to perform before people. We were like that. The writer saw the press conference.

Paul McCartney: I was in a film. I don't care what they picture me as. So far as I'm concerned I'm just doing a job in a film. If the film calls for me to be a cheerful chap, well, great; I'll be a cheerful chap.

It does seem to have fallen in my role to be kind of a bit more that than others. I was always known in the Beatle thing as being the one who would kind of sit the press down and say, "Hello, how are you? Do you want a drink?" and make them comfortable. I guess that's me. My family loop was like that. So I kind of used to do that, plus a little more polished than I might normally have done, but you're aware you're talking to the press. . . . You want a good article, don't you, so you don't want to go sluggin' the guys off.

But I'm not ashamed of anything I've been, you know. I kind of like the idea of doing sometimes and if it turn out in a few years to look a bit sloppy I'd say, "Oh well, sloppy. So what?" I think most people dig it. You get people livin' out in Queens or say Red Creek, Minnesota, and they're all wiped out themselves . . . you know, ordinary people. Once you get into the kind of critical bit, people analysing you and then you start to look at yourself and start to analyse yourself, and you think, oh Christ, you got me, and things start to rebound on ya, why didn't I put on a kind of smart image . . . you know, why wasn't I kind of tougher? I'm not really tough. I'm not really lovable, either, but I don't mind falling in the middle. My dad's advice: moderation, son. Every father in the world tells you moderation.

Can we look forward to any more Beatle movies?
John: Well, there'll be many more but I don't know whether you can look forward to them or not.

When are you starting your next movie?
Paul: In February.
George: We have no title for it yet.
Ringo: We have no story for it yet.
John: We have no actors for it yet.

Are you going to have a leading lady in the film you are about to make?
Paul: We're trying to get the Queen. She sells in England, you know.

Help!

John Lennon: *Help* was a drag, because we didn't know what was happening. In fact Lester was a bit ahead of his time with the Batman thing, but we were on pot by then and all the best stuff is on the cutting-room floor, with us breaking up and falling about all over the place.

Magical Mystery Tour.

John Lennon: Paul made an attempt to carry on as if Brian hadn't died by saying, "Now, now, boys, we're going to make a record." Being the kind of person I am, I thought well, we're going to make a record all right, so I'll go along, so we went and made a record. And that's when we made *Magical Mystery Tour.* That was the real . . .

Paul had a tendency to come along and say well he's written these ten songs, let's record now. And I said, "Well, give us a few days, and I'll knock a few off," or something like that. *Magical Mystery Tour* was something he had worked out with Mal and he showed me what his idea was and this is how it went, it went around like this, the story and how he had it all . . . the production and everything.

Paul said, "Well, here's the segment, you write a little piece for that," and I thought "Bloody hell," so I ran off and I wrote the dream sequence for the fat woman and all the thing with the spaghetti. Then George and I were sort of grumbling about the fuckin' movie and we thought we better do it and we had the feeling that we owed it to the public to do these things.

Paul McCartney: I learned how easy it is to get very involved in everything. You've got to see it right through. But you also get too involved in union problems. You have to spend so much time getting round their rules, without offending them.

We were lucky in the end with the technicians, but you should organise them better so that they are the sort who can fit in with improvised methods.

But you've got to improvise. It's no use waiting for days for the sun to come out, just because you've decided you want a sunny shot, the way film people do. What's there already is what you want. Films should be elastic.

It was really just like making a record album, that's how we did it, anyway. We just got a lot of things ready and fitted them together. A record is sound and a film is visual, that's the only difference. In the future all records will have vision as well as sound. In twenty years' time people will be amazed to think we just listened to records.

We didn't worry about the fact that we didn't know anything about making films and had never

STILL FROM HELP!

111

made one before. We realised years ago you don't need knowledge in this world to do anything. All you need is sense, whatever that is. The film was not shown in the USA . . .

At the time, "Hey," I thought, "Oh, blimey," but . . . eh . . . it started out to be one of those kind of things. Like *The Wild One*, you know Marlon Brando . . . at the time it couldn't be released. The interest in it came later. The interest started to grow, you know. *Magical Mystery Tour* was a bit like than . . . well, whatever happened to it . . . that's a bit magical

itself, like the Stones' *Rock and Roll Circus*. You know, what happened to that, you know. I mean, I'd like to see that. So all of those things work out well. You've got to be patient. Everything like that works out well. I think it was a good show. It will have its day, you know.

Let It Be.

John Lennon: It was hell making the film *Let It Be*. When it came out a lot of people complained about Yoko looking miserable in it. But even the biggest Beatle fan couldn't have sat through those six weeks of misery. It was the most miserable session on earth.

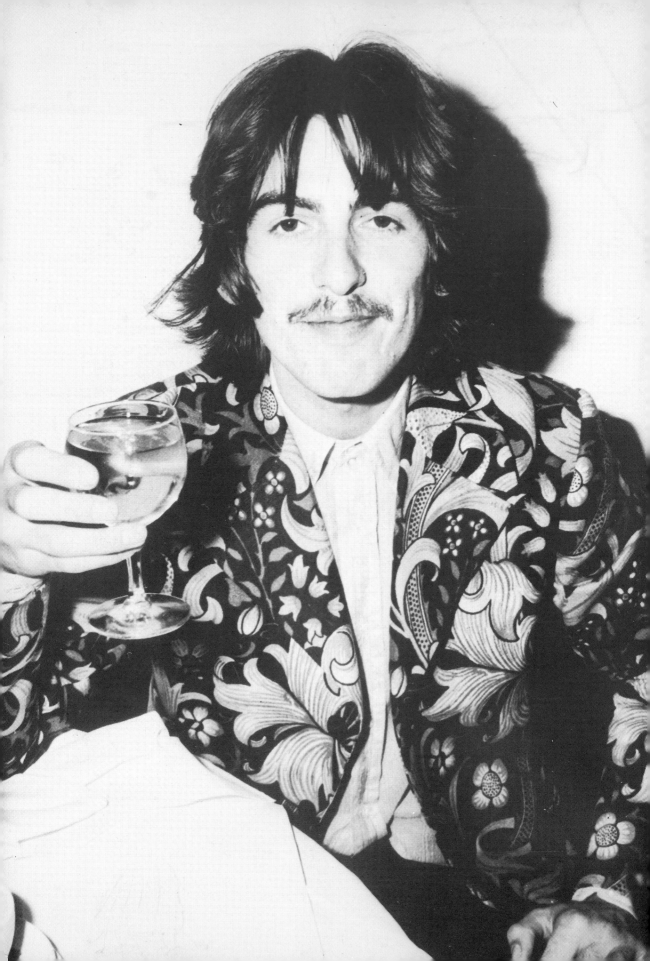

Drugs.

John Lennon: In *A Hard Day's Night* I was on pills, that's drugs, that's bigger drugs than pot. Started on pills when I was 15, no, since I was 17, since I became a musician. The only way to survive in Hamburg, to play eight hours a night, was to take pills. The waiters gave you them — the pills and drink. I was a fucking dropped-down drunk in art school. *Help* was where we turned on to pot and we dropped drink, simple as that. I've always needed a drug to survive. The others, too, but I always had more, more pills, more of everything because I'm more crazy probably.

What are your feelings about LSD?
Paul McCartney: I don't recommend it. It can open a few doors but it's not any answer. You get the answers yourself.

John Lennon: A dentist in London laid it on George, me and wives, without telling us, at a dinner party at his house. He was a friend of George's and our dentist at the time, and he just put it in our coffee or something. He didn't know what it was; it's all the same thing with that sort of middle class London swinger, or whatever. They had all heard about it, and they didn't know it was different from pot or pills and they gave us it. He said "I advise you not to leave," and we all thought he was trying to keep us for an orgy in his house, and we didn't want to know, and we went to the Ad Lib and these discotheques and there were these incredible things going on.

It was insane going around London. When we went to the club we thought it was on fire and then we thought it was a première, and it was just an ordinary light outside. We thought, "Shit, what's going on here?" We were cackling in the streets, and people were shouting "Let's break a window," you know, it was just insane. We were just out of our heads. When we finally got on the lift we all thought there was a fire, but there was just a little red light. We were all screaming like that, and we were all hot and hysterical, and when we all arrived on the floor, because this was a discotheque that was up a building, the lift stopped and the door opened and we were all screaming.

I had read somebody describing the effects of opium in the old days and I thought "Fuck! It's happening," and then we went to the Ad Lib and all of that, and then some singer came up to me and said, "Can I sit next to you?" And I said,

"Only if you don't talk," because I just couldn't think.

This seemed to go on all night. I can't remember the details. George somehow or another managed to drive us home in his mini. We were going about ten miles an hour, but it seemed like a thousand and Patti was saying let's jump out and play football. I was getting all these sort of hysterical jokes coming out like speed, because I was always on that, too.

God, it was just terrifying, but it was fantastic. I did some drawings at the time, I've got them somewhere, of four faces saying "We all agree with you!" I gave them to Ringo, the originals. I did a lot of drawing that night. And then George's house seemed to be just like a big submarine, I was driving it, they all went to bed, I was carrying on in it, it seemed to float above his wall which was 18 foot and I was driving it.

I was pretty stoned for a month or two. The second time we had it was in L.A. We were on tour in one of those houses, Doris Day's house or wherever it was we used to stay, and the three of us took it, Ringo, George and I. Maybe Neil and a couple of the Byrds — what's his name, the one in the Stills and Nash thing, Crosby and the other guy, who used to do the lead. McGuinn. I think they came, I'm not sure, on a few trips. But there was a reporter, Don Short. We were in the garden, it was only our second one and we still didn't know anything about doing it in a nice place and cool it. Then they saw the reporter and thought "How do we act?" We were terrified waiting for him to go, and he wondered why we couldn't come over. Neil, who never had acid either, had taken it and he would have to play road manager, and we said go get rid of Don Short, and he didn't know what to do.

Peter Fonda came, and that was another thing. He kept saying "I know what it's like to be dead," and we said "What?" and he kept saying it. We were saying "For Christ's sake, shut up, we don't care, we don't want to know," and he kept going on about it. That's how I wrote 'She Said, She Said' — "I know what it's like to be dead." It was a sad song, an acidy song I suppose. "When I was a little boy" . . . you see, a lot of early childhood was coming out, anyway.

It went on for years, I must have had a thousand trips.

A thousand. I used to just eat it all the time. I never took it in the studio. Once I thought I

was taking some uppers and I was not in the state of handling it, I can't remember what album it was, but I took it and I just noticed . . . I suddenly got so scared on the mike. I thought I felt ill, and I thought I was going to crack. I said I must get some air. They all took me upstairs on the roof and George Martin was looking at me funny, and then it dawned on me I must have taken acid. I said, "Well I can't go on, you'll have to do it and I'll just stay and watch." You know I got very nervous just watching them all. I was saying, "Is it all right?" And they were saying, "Yeah." They had all been very kind and they carried on making the record.

In L.A. the second time we took it, Paul felt very out of it, because we are all a bit slightly cruel, sort of "we're taking it, and *you're* not." But we kept *seeing him,* you know. We couldn't eat our food, I just couldn't manage it, just picking it up with our hands. There were all these people serving us in the house and we were knocking food on the floor and all of that. It was a long time before Paul took it. Then there was the big announcement.

So, I think George was pretty heavy on it; we are probably the most cracked. Paul is a bit more stable than George and I.

I think LSD profoundly shocked him, and Ringo. I think maybe they *regret* it.

I had many bad trips, Jesus Christ, I stopped taking it because of that. I just couldn't stand it.

I stopped it for I don't know how long, and then I started taking it again just before I met Yoko. Derek came over and . . . you see, I got the message that I should destroy my ego and I did, you know. I was reading that stupid book of Leary's; we were going through a whole game that everybody went through, and I destroyed myself. I was slowly putting myself together round about Maharishi time. Bit by bit over a two-year period, I had destroyed me ego.

I didn't believe I could do anything and let people make me, and let them all just do what they wanted. I just was nothing. I was shit. Then Derek tripped me out at his house after he got back from L.A. He sort of said "You're all right," and pointed out which songs I had written. "You wrote this," and "You said this" and "You are intelligent, don't be frightened."

The next week I went to Derek's with Yoko and we tripped again, and she filled me completely to realize that I was me and that it's all right. That was it; I started fighting again, being a loudmouth again and saying, "I *can* do this, fuck it, this is what I want, you know, I want it and don't put me down," I did this, so that's where I am now.

The two years before I met Yoko — I think the others were going through the same thing — of real big depression after Maharishi, and Brian dying. It wasn't really to do with Maharishi, it

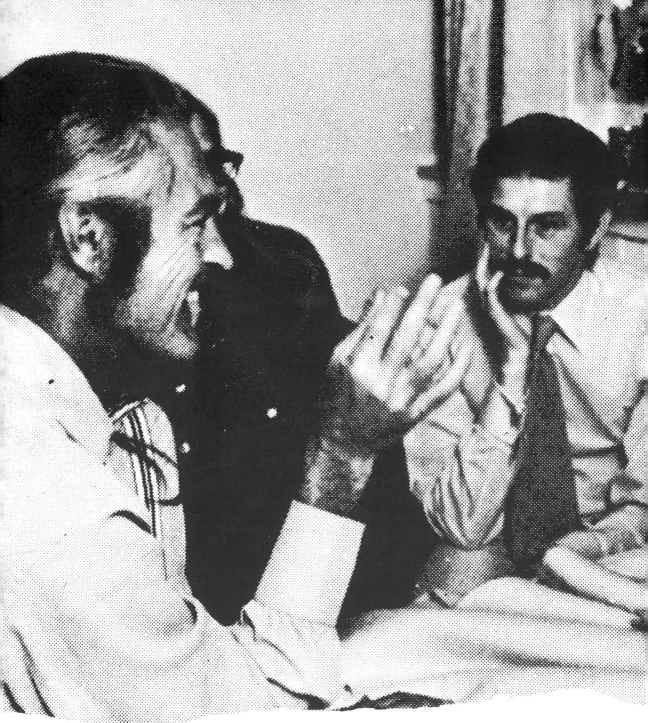

was just that period, I was really going through a "What's it all about? This song-writing is nothing, it's pointless and I'm no good, not talented and I'm a shit and I couldn't do anything but be a Beatle and what am I going to do about . . ." And it lasted nearly two years! I was still in it in *Pepper*! I know Paul wasn't at that time: he was feeling full of confidence but I wasn't. I was going through murder around those periods. I was just about coming out of it around Maharishi, even though Brian had died and that

knocked us back again, with the acid trip scene we all went through. That "Trying to get rid of your ego" bit. So I really had a massive ego and for three or four years after that I spent the time trying to destroy my ego — until I had nothing left! And I went to India with Maharishi and that and he was saying: "Ego is good as long as you look after it" and I had really destroyed it and I was so paranoiac and weak I couldn't do anything. I had really done a good job on my ego! I was just about building it up again when I met Yoko. I was trying to build it back up again and get confidence in myself and we met Derek

118

again after a long time. Derek [Taylor] did a good job building me ego one weekend at his house, reminding me who I am and what I had done and what I could do, and he and a couple of friends did that for me. They sort of said, "You're great! You are what you are!" and all that and then the next week Yoko came down to Derek's and that was it then. I just blew out! It all came back to me like I was back to age 16. All the rest of it had been wiped out. It was like going through psychiatry really. I've got to

believe in my genius. I've got to believe I'm great — great to do anything. I believe it, it's my mantra, and of course I lose it all and I really don't believe in genius for when those readers read it, just to cover that angle! If there is a genius then I am one and if there isn't I don't believe in them. It's just when it comes in print and it says: "I am a genius, I am great" it depresses me if it's read the wrong way. Like one of the criticisms of the film event, I don't remember which paper. He didn't know us and hadn't followed my career or Yoko's. He thought we were on a big ego trip with the films of my face but he realised that it isn't just that, now it's just coming over to him. So that's a danger we've got to watch out for. The thing was coming out and she [Yoko] really opened the door by saying, "I love you for what you are and whatever it is" and I respected her genius and for her to love me was the answer then! She wouldn't have loved a dummy which I was beginning to think I was. That helped. I was just out of it. Of course she goes through the same thing but I can help her the same way. Once I got over my intellectual-reverse-snobbery about "avant garde" and that sort of thing which I had to get over.

Paul McCartney: God is in everything. God is in the space between us. God is in the table in front of you. It just happens I realise all this through acid. It could have been through anything else.

George Harrison: Although we've been identified a lot with hippies, especially since all this thing about pot and LSD's come out, we don't want to tell anyone else to have it because it's something that's up to the person himself. Although it was like a key that opened the door and showed a lot of things on the other side, it's still up to people themselves what they do with it.

LSD isn't a real answer. It doesn't give you anything. It enables you to see a lot of possibilities that you may never have noticed before, but it isn't the answer. You don't just take LSD and that's it forever, you're OK.

A hippie is supposed to be someone who becomes aware — you're hip if you know what's going on. But if you're really hip you don't get involved with LSD and things like that. You see the potential that it has and the good that can come from it, but you also see that you don't really need it.

I needed it the first time I ever had it. Actually, I didn't know that I'd had it, I'd never heard of it then. This is something that just hasn't been told. Everybody now knows that we've had it but the circumstances were that somebody just shoved it into our coffee before we'd ever heard of the stuff. So we happened to have it quite unaware of the fact.

I don't mind telling people I've had it. I'm not embarrassed. It makes no difference because I know that I didn't actually go out and try to get some.

. . . It can help you to go from A to B, but when you get to B, you see C. And you see that to get really high, you have to go it straight. There are special ways of getting high without drugs — with yoga, meditation, and all those things. So this was the disappointing thing about LSD.

In the physical world we live in, there's always duality — good and bad, black and white, yes and no. Whatever there is, there's always the opposite. There's always something equal and opposite to everything, and this is why you can't say LSD is good or it's bad because it's good AND it's bad. It's both of them and it's neither of them all together. People don't consider that.

. . . I don't mind anybody dropping out of anything, but it's the imposition on somebody else I don't like. The moment you start dropping out and then begging off somebody else to help you — then it's no good. I've just realised through a lot of things that it doesn't matter what you are as long as you work. It doesn't matter if you chop wood — as long as you chop and keep chopping. Then you get what's coming to you. You don't have to drop out. In fact, if you drop out you put yourself further away from the goal of life than if you were to keep working.

. . . We've all got the same goal whether we realise it or not. We're all striving for something which is called God. For a reunion, complete. Everybody has realised at some time or other that no matter how happy they are, there's still always the unhappiness that comes with it.

Everyone is a potential Jesus Christ, really. We are all trying to get to where Jesus Christ got. And we're going to be on this world until we get there. We're all different people and we are all doing different things in life, but that doesn't matter because the whole point of life is to harmonise with everything, every aspect in creation. That means down to not killing the flies, eating the meat, killing people or chopping the trees down.

. . . Everybody is potentially divine. It's just a matter of self-realisation before it will all happen. The hippies are a good idea — love, flowers and that is great — but when you see the other half of it, it's like anything. I love all these people too, those who are honest and trying to find a bit of truth and to straighten out the untruths. I'm with them 100% but when I see the bad side of it, I'm not so happy.

. . . The Beatles got all the material wealth that we needed, and that was enough to show us that this thing wasn't material. We are all in the physical world, yet what we are striving for isn't physical. We all get so hung up with material things like cars and televisions and houses, yet what they can give you is only there for a little bit and then it's gone.

. . . I'm a musician. I don't know why. This is a thing that I've looked back on since my birth. Many people feel that life is pre-destined. I think it is vaguely, but it's still up to you which way your life's going to go. All I've ever done is to keep being me and it's just all worked out. It just did it all . . . magic . . . it just did it. We never planned anything. So it's obvious — because I'm a musician now, that's what I was destined to be. It's my gig.

Politics.

Why are you disinterested in politics?
John: We're not. We just think politicians are disinteresting.
What do you think of the Vietnam war?
John: We think of it every day. We don't like it. We don't agree with it. We think it's wrong. But there is not much we can do about it. All we can do is say we don't like it.
What is your opinion of Americans who go to Canada to avoid the draft?
John: We're not allowed opinions.
Paul: Anyone who feels that fighting is wrong has the right not to go in the army.
John: We all just don't agree with war. There's no need for anyone to kill for any reason.
George: "Thou shalt not kill" means *that* — not, "Amend section A". There's no reason whatsoever. No one can force you to kill anyone if you don't want to.

John Lennon: I enjoyed it when football crowds in the early days would sing 'All Together Now'. I was also pleased when the movement in America took up 'Give Peace A Chance' because I had written it with that in mind really. I hoped that instead of singing 'We Shall Overcome' from 1800 or something, they would have something contemporary. I felt an obligation even then to write a song that people would sing in the pub or on a demonstration. That is why I would like to compose songs for the revolution now . . .

Even during the Beatle heyday I tried to go against it, so did George. We went to America a few times and Epstein always tried to waffle on at us about saying nothing about Vietnam. So there came a time when George and I said "Listen, when they ask next time, we're going to say that we don't like that war and we think they should get right out." That's what we did. At that time this was a pretty radical thing to do, especially for the "Fab Four". It was the first opportunity I personally took to wave the flag a bit. But you've got to remember that I'd always felt repressed. We were all so pressurized that there was hardly any chance of expressing ourselves, especially working at that rate, touring continually and always kept in a cocoon of myths and dreams. It's pretty hard when you are Caesar and everyone is saying how wonderful you are and they are giving you all the goodies and the girls, it's pretty hard to break out of that to say, "Well, I don't want to be king, I want to

be real." So in its way the second political thing I did was to say "The Beatles are bigger than Jesus." That really broke the scene. I nearly got shot in America for that. It was a big trauma for all the kids that were following us. Up to then there was this unspoken policy of not answering delicate questions, though I always read the papers, you know, the political bits. The continual awareness of what was going on made me feel ashamed I wasn't saying anything. I burst out because I could no longer play that game any more, it was just too much for me. Of course, going to America increased the build up on me, especially as the war was going on there. In a way we'd turned out to be a Trojan Horse. The "Fab Four" moved right to the top and then sang about drugs and sex and then I got more and more into the heavy stuff and that's when they started dropping us.

John Lennon: I've always been politically minded, you know, and against the status quo. It's pretty basic when you're brought up, like I was, to hate and fear the police as a natural enemy and to despise the army as something that takes everybody away and leaves them dead somewhere. I mean, it's just a basic working class thing, though it begins to wear off when you get older, get a family and get swallowed up in the system. In my case I've never not been political, though religion tended to overshadow it in my acid days; that would be around '65 and '66. And that religion was directly the result of all that superstar shit-religion was an outlet for my repression. I thought, "Well, there's something else to life, isn't there? This isn't it, surely?" But I was always political in a way, you know. In the two books I wrote, even though they were written in a sort of Joycean gobbledygook, there's many knocks at religion and there is a play about a worker and a capitalist. I've been satirizing the system since my childhood. I used to write magazines in school and hand them around. I was very conscious of class, they would say with a chip on my shoulder, because I knew what happened to me and I knew about the class repression coming down on us — it was a fucking fact but in the hurricane Beatle world it got left out — I got farther away from reality for a time.

What did you think was the reason for the success of your sort of music?
John: Well, at that time it was thought that the

workers had broken through, but I realize in retrospect that it's the same phoney deal they give to blacks, it was just like they allowed blacks to be runners or boxers or entertainers. That's the choice they allow you — now the outlet is being a pop star, which is really what I'm saying in 'Working Class Hero'. As I told

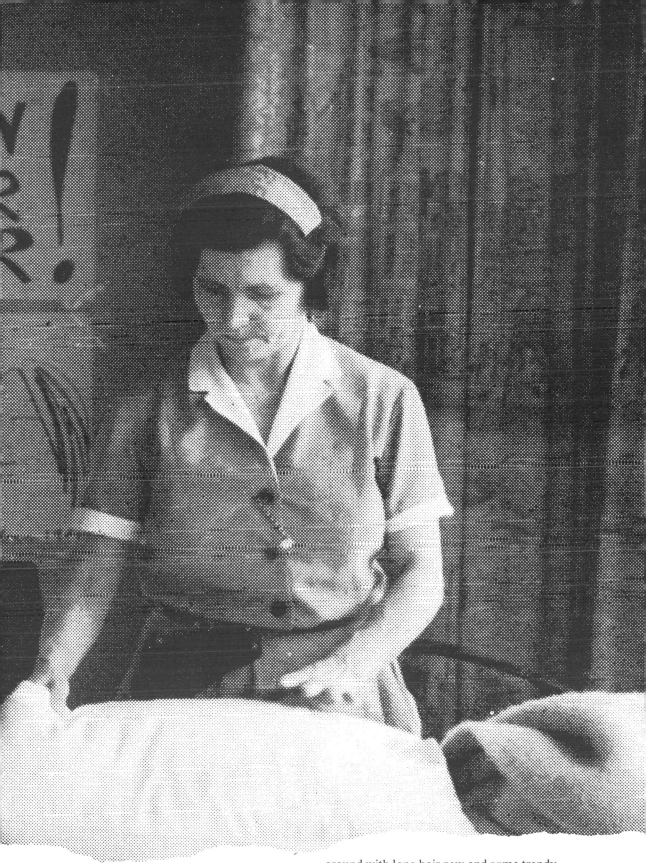

Rolling Stone, it's the same people who have power, the class system didn't change one little bit. Of course there are a lot of people walking around with long hair now and some trendy middle class kids in pretty clothes. But nothing changed except that we all dressed up a bit, leaving the same bastards running everything.

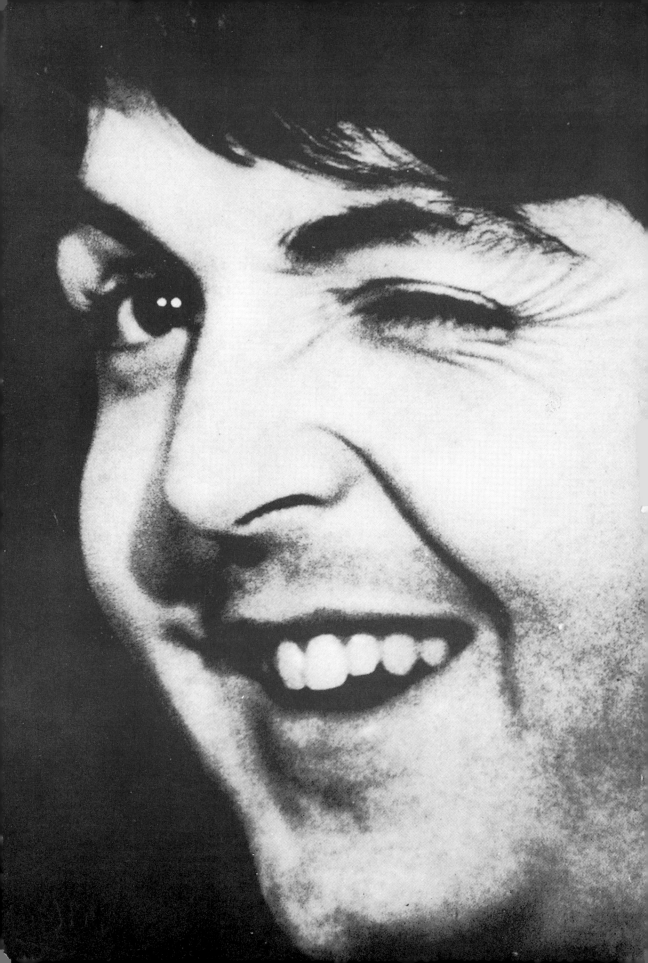